Tooppil Bhaasi

Memories in Hiding

NEW INDIAN PLAYWRIGHTS

Badal Sircar	*Beyond the Land of Hattamala and Scandal in Fairyland*
Vijay Tendulkar	*Ghashiram Kotwal*
Mahesh Elkunchwar	*Two Plays*
Mahesh Elkunchwar	*Party*
Mahesh Elkunchwar	*Old Stone Mansion*
Mahesh Elkunchwar	*Autobiography*
Satish Alekar	*The Dread Departure*
Satish Alekar	*Begum Barve*
Chandrasekhar Kambar	*Jokumaraswami*
Chandrasekhar Kambar	*Samba Shiva: A Farce*
Chandrasekhar Kambar	*Siri Sampige*
K. N. Panikkar	*The Right to Rule and The Domain of the Sun*
K. N. Panikkar	*Karimkutty and The Lone Tusker*
Shanta Gokhale	*Avinash*
G. P. Deshpande	*A Man in Dark Times*
G. P. Deshpande	*Past One o'Clock*
Mrinal Pande	*That Which Ram Hath Ordained or The Tale of Manna Seth*
Habib Tanvir	*Charandas Chor*

PERFORMANCE TEXTS

Rustom Bharucha	*The Theatre of Kanhailal: Pebet & Memoirs of Africa*

Also available:

Anuradha Kapur	*Actors, Pilgrims, Kings and Gods: The Ramlila at Ramnagar*
Richard Schechner	*Performative Circumstances from the Avant Garde to Ramlila*
David Hays	*Light on the Subject*

Memories in Hiding
(Olivile Ormmakal)

Tooppil Bhaasi

Translated from the original Malayalam by
Jose George and Phillip B. Zarrilli

Seagull Books
CALCUTTA 1996

Amminiamma Toopil,
Vallikunnam P.O.
Alleppey District,
Kerala 690 501.
Telephone 0478-335224

Cover design by
Naveen Kishore

ISBN 81 7046 134 0

*Published by Naveen Kishore, Seagull Books
26 Circus Avenue, Calcutta 700017*

*Printed in India by Laurens & Co.
9 Crooked Lane, Calcutta 700 069*

Contents

ACKNOWLEDGEMENTS

First, the translators wish to thank Tooppil Bhaasi's wife, Amminiamma, and his son, Ajayan, for their permission to publish this translation.

We also wish to thank the Secretary and company members of the Kerala People's Arts Club who so graciously gave of their time, energy, and hospitality while attending performances of *Memories in Hiding*, as well as other plays in their repertory, and for giving extensive interviews. This translation would never have been undertaken without their assistance and enthusiasm.

Thanks also to Professor V. R. Prabodhachandran Nayar of the University of Kerala for his assistance with the translation of the songs and their poetic imagery.

All photographs are by Phillip B. Zarrilli and Sharon A. Grady. They were taken at several performances of *Memories in Hiding* between March and September 1993.

Phillip Zarrilli wishes to acknowledge, with thanks, research funds provided by Fulbright and Guggenheim Fellowships which allowed him to work on this project.

Note on editorial additions: For the reader unfamiliar with specific references, we have added to Bhaasi's text numerous explanatory footnotes. Original stage directions are in parentheses.

Note on Transliteration: Although a complete system of transliteration is not followed here, to assist in pronunciation, long vowels are indicated by doubling, such as 'oo' and 'aa' in 'Tooppil Bhaasi'.

ABOUT THE TRANSLATORS

DR JOSE GEORGE received his Ph.D. in Theatre from the University of Calicut School of Drama. He is a recipient of a pre-doctoral Fulbright Fellowship for study in the United States. A prolific researcher and author, his essays have appeared in journals both in India and the USA.

PHILLIP B. ZARRILLI is currently Professor and Chair, Department of Theatre Arts and Dance, California State University, Los Angeles, USA. He has been coming to Kerala since 1976 and has researched, written about, and trained extensively in *kalarippayattu* and *kathakali*. He is author of *The Kathakali Complex* (New Delhi: Abhinav, 1984), *When 'The Body Becomes All Eyes': Kalarippayattu, a Traditional Martial and Medical System of Kerala, South India* (in press), and co-author with Farley Richmond and Darius Swann of *Indian Theatre* (Honolulu University of Hawaii Press, 1990).

TOOPPIL BHAASI'S THEATRE OF SOCIAL CONSCIENCE AND THE KERALA PEOPLE'S ARTS CLUB

> KPAC [Kerala People's Art's Club] became a very powerful social inspiration for people to fight against social injustice and for their rights. It gave them the feeling that anybody, irrespective of their low birth or high birth, are all equal—Dr Radhakrishnan (Gandhi Center, New Delhi).[1]

Tooppil Bhaasi was born to Tooppil Parameswaran Pillai and Nanukkutti Anna on April 8, 1924 in Vallikkunu, Allappuzha District, south central Kerala–part of the old central Travancore region. Bhaasi received his lower school education in Vallikkunnam SNDP Sanskrit School, and in the Changankulangara School. He later went on to pass his Sastri examination, and received his 'Vaidya Kala Nidhi' from the Government Ayurveda College, Thiruvananthapuram for the practice of Ayurvedic medicine.

However, Bhaasi never pursued a career in indigenous medicine. Rather, while a student at the Ayurvedic College he became a political activist and leader, first working in the student Congress movement, and later in the communist movement. By Independence Day (August 15, 1947), he was in the Allappuzha jail. From 1948 through 1952 he continued his revolutionary political activities and often lived in hiding.

Beginning as early as the 1930's, during Kerala's formative political years, progressive thinkers, a number of whom, like Bhaasi, were from the educated higher castes and communities and who joined the Communist Party of India (CPI), helped foster both a desire for awareness and a reassessment of the social ills of the old feudalistic order. To accomplish this goal, political parties and special interest organizations have had a long history of fostering educational, cultural, and artistic activities, usually under the guidance of the party or organization's 'cultural wing.' As early as the founding of the Congress Socialist Party in 1934, new dramas (*puthiya naatakam*) were performed as one strategy of leftist/socialist political education.[2] When the Kerala branch of the CPI was born in 1939-40, along with other socialist parties it helped establish literacy programs in the form of reading rooms which made available modern literary works of members of the

---

1 Personal interview, June 26, 1993.

2 T. J. Nossiter, *Marxist State Governments in India* (London, 1988), 47–8.

Progressive Writer's Association 'in whose work social criticism dominated', such as Kesava Dev's *From the Gutter* (1942), and Thakazhi's *Scavenger's Son* (1947) and *Two Measures of Rice* (1948).[3] The cultural wing of the Kerala branch of the CPI began to use social dramas both to raise consciousness about social ills, and to propagate potential socialist solutions for these ills, a strategy which helped prepare the way for Bhaasi's involvement in leftist social drama.

While he was in hiding in 1952 his first play, *You Made Me a Communist*, was produced by KPAC. KPAC was founded in 1950 by a group of committed student activists at the Law College in Ernakulam when they first used a shadow puppet play as one means of raising socio-political issues. In 1951 they wrote and staged their own play, *My Son is Right*; however, the production was unable to create the type of popular public response for which they had hoped. Apparently inspired by *My Son is Right*, while in prison Tooppil Bhaasi wrote *You Made Me a Communist*, which appeared in print under the pen name Soman. Members of KPAC read Bhaasi's play, and then approached him for permission to stage it.

Their 1952 production of *You Made Me a Communist* helped sensitize a generation of Malayalis to issues of social conscience, and helped initiate a mass modern theatre movement throughout the state of Kerala. Since then, *You Made Me a Communist* has been performed by KPAC more than 2,000 times, and continues to be performed today as part of its repertory. Indeed, it may be the longest continuously running popular political drama in the history of the modern theatre.[4]

Although KPAC, today's most popular and often-booked professional theatre group in Kerala, has two companies each of which performs as many or more than 300 times each year, is affiliated with the Indian People's Theatre Association (IPTA), has spawned a number of other professional theatre companies which also produce social dramas (Omasanan's Kalidasa Kalakendra, Sulochana's Samskara, and N. N. Pillai's Vishwakalakendra), and has produced a number of Kerala's most popular cinema actors, we need to remember that the original actors in the 1952 production were not professionals, but dedicated and active political workers seeking to spread their messages of social reform and revolution through drama.

In the context of the dominant form of contemporary theatre in the early 1950's—the Tamil music-drama tradition of enacting epic and puranic stories—Bhaasi's *You Made Me a Communist* not only had a

---

3 T.J. Nossiter, *Communism in Kerala* (Delhi, 1982), 95.

4 The number of performances of *You Made Me a Communist* each year has diminished from almost daily performances in 1952-4 to four in 1993. Among those four 1993 performances, *You Made Me a Communist* was staged for the CPI all-India meet in March, 1993. Obviously the impact and reception of the play has changed over the years.

revolutionary social message, but was part of a revolution in representation. Instead of larger-than-life epic characters, 'real' everyday people and their immediate and very pressing concerns were brought to the stage. But other leftist dramas had also attempted to focus attention on 'real' everyday people. Part of what made *You Made Me a Communist* unique was when O. N. V. Kurup and Devarajan collaborated with KPAC by adding thirteen original songs and music to the production. The combination of popular music with the dramatization of timely social issues not only put everyday people and their concerns on the stage, but provided political activists with rousing, memorable, and singable songs.[5]

The content, songs, and timely everyday concerns created an immediate and widespread demand for performances of *You Made Me a Communist*. Dr Radhakrishnan recalls the fervour and pitched excitement prompted by KPAC's *You Made Me a Communist*: 'Even though a child, I could see the excitement. There were nights when KPAC had more than four performances. From one place they will go on moving for months together. For months they were completely booked.'

The play was not only popular and topical, but potentially dangerous. Since the movement was banned, and many of the players, like Bhaasi himself, were in hiding from the police, once a performance was over, the performers not only left the stage, but had to disappear into the countryside so that they wouldn't be apprehended. Seventy-eight year old Ganesha Iyer, a teacher at the time, recalls how anyone attached to the government didn't want to risk seeing the play [for fear of retribution or loss of one's job]. 'But I went. I was free from politics, so nobody could find fault with me for seeing the play. But most of my colleagues would not see this or other plays for fear that they would be dubbed a communist.'[6]

There can be no doubt that there was a decided sense of 'eventness' to attending a performance of *You Made Me a Communist* in 1952-3–it was not simply a dramatic representation of a fictionalized story and its characters, but part of an unfolding and evolving socio-political revolution *as it was happening*. Journalist, essayist, playwright and activist Kaniyapuram Ramachandran explains both the timeliness and excitement generated by this interrelationship between stage and 'life' in Bhaasi's early social dramas, and in *You Made Me a Communist* in particular:

The fourth element of drama is the audience; and the audience is the

---

5 These songs have become a hallmark feature of many KPAC productions, and the audio-cassette of these popular songs are available in cassette shops throughout Kerala. Sometimes music is also used for 'local colour' to represent specific castes/classes, as in *Memories in Hiding*.

6 Personal interview, July 14, 1993.

> fourth character. That dividing line between stage and audience was simply erased! What they saw there was their real lives! The workers, agricultural labourers, people coming onstage and speaking *their own dialects and ordinary language*—not literary language. The ultimate aim is to make the audience part of the experience. There is no detachment, but attachment. So with the social issues in the play—it was all so relevant. At the end of a performance the entire audience would come to its feet.
>
> So, *You Made Me a Communist* wasn't a drama at all! The social relevance of the play made people forget everything when they saw it. It was a drama for the people, by the people. It gave people what they wanted to see at the right time. It was a magic wand. The audience was like a mental vacuum that sucked up what was given . . . In 1951 it was so apt! It was the medicine that the patient was waiting for. People were ready for that message of social change.
>
> Bhaasi always wanted the audience to first understand his plays. They should be clear and straight. He was speaking to the heart, and not the intellect. He used to talk to the emotions, and through the emotions, people would change their thinking.[7]

So important a role did KPAC and this production play in the popular spread of the communist point of view during 1952-4 that some commentators have suggested that the election of the communists in 1957 would never have happened without the impact that this production had on the political concerns and popular imaginations of Malayalis during the 1950s.

Officially affiliated with and financially supported by the CPI, by 1955 KPAC began to expand its repertory to include new plays authored by Bhaasi which focused on other issues of social conscience, among which the most notable, popular, and enduring have been *The Prodigal Son* (*Mutiyanaaya Puutran*, 1956), and *Ashwameetam* (1962). *The Prodigal Son* plays out struggles over caste, class, and economics as a wayward son, representing the younger generation of land-holding families within the feudal structure, eventually is transformed from a selfish rowdy and womanizer into an enlightened champion of the low caste Pulayans who are the only ones to befriend him and provide him succour when in need.

In *Ashwameetam* Bhaasi opened up another controversial subject which had never been brought to the stage before—leprosy—when a young woman about to be married suddenly contracts this dreaded disease and herself, at least temporarily, becomes an outcaste. Like her male counterpart in *The Prodigal Son*, the heroine in *Ashwameetam*

---

7 Personal interview, June 11, 1993.

undergoes a transformation of social conscience from her experience of being an outsider, specifically in her views of those 'cast out' by society—lepers or lower castes. Just as significant is the fact that at the end of the play the heroine chooses to remain single and dedicate herself to nursing rather than becoming a wife.

Over the years, KPAC actors under Bhaasi's direction developed a distinctive style which M. Gopi, current General Secretary of KPAC, explains as actualizing the 'everyday' on stage:

> We don't adopt an artificial style of acting. It should be natural. Bhaasi was very particular about that. He trained the actors for this. He would say, 'You shouldn't imagine you're on the stage. It should be like you're speaking in your house.'[8]

The collective effect of Bhaasi's early social dramas, their focus on 'real life' problems, and KPAC's acting them as 'naturally' as possible was comparable to the revolution in European drama brought about by Ibsen's plays.

> The theme of *Ashwameetam* was as powerful and as severe in terms of its evocative images and the manner in which it went to the hearts of the audience, as was the moment when Nora walked out of her husband's house slamming the door! It had the same kind of impact [on Malayalam drama].[9]

However, one proviso is necessary. Although Bhaasi's characters and situations are taken from 'real' life, and the actors are supposed to act 'naturally' as in everyday life, here 'real' and 'natural' refer not to the underlying 'realism' of the psychological paradigm which keeps the focus of Ibsen's (and other Western realist dramas) on individual characters and their motivations, but rather to the simple fact that these are the 'real' stories of 'real' people you might meet on the street. Indeed, some plays, like *Memories in Hiding*, are based on actual people and 'real' events. They are also 'real' in *contrast* to the fantastic gods, heroes/heroines, and demons of the epics and puranas of the old Tamil music-drama stage, or of today's *kathakali* and *kutiyattam* performances. They are 'real' because they wear everyday dress, speak a colloquial language and dialects, behave in a distinctively recognizable manner that is identifiable by caste and/or class, sing folk songs and dance folk dances, and act with the traditional prejudices and/or opinions one expects of those who are landlords or politicians. 'Real' means that the characters and what they do are situated within a commonplace network of expectations and behaviour associated with the way Malayalis stereotypically organize themselves within traditional society, and which are therefore open to question and revision. For example, in

---

8 Personal interview, June 9, 1993.
9 Dr Radhakrishnan interview.

Memories in Hiding, the Pulayan field-worker, Ceennan, displays absolute deference to the landlord (Janmi) at the beginning of the play. This is the 'reality' of the relationship between traditional feudal landlords and their 'slaves'. It is not important in the drama to flesh out the underlying motivations for the characters' actions toward one another. It is sufficient that their behaviors and attitudes be clearly shown so that the transformation of Ceennan's social conscience and politics by the end of the play is demonstrated.

Unlike Ibsenesque realism in which stereotypes and caricatures are banished in favor of the subtle inflections of psychologically-motivated behaviour and actions, in Bhaasi's social dramas easily-recognizable, and usually comic caricatures and stereotypes often appear as a counterbalance to the more serious characters who undergo a transformation of conscience and therefore of behaviour, attitude, and, by implication, of point of view, world view, and therefore of politics. Among Bhaasi's many memorable caricatures is the ridiculous antique-of-a-man—the stiff-backed, white-haired Congress MLA of *The Prodigal Son* who hopelessly and ridiculously fawns over the beautiful young woman of the Pulayan family, or the same play's equally remarkable send-up of the *mantra vadyan* who performs his 'meaningless' incantations and ritual actions. These caricatures are part of Bhaasi's astute sense of 'the theatrical possibilities of the stage'. As playwright K.T. Mohammed explains, Bhaasi 'never wrote a play as a piece of literature, but only for the stage.' Mohammed cites the example of *Memories in Hiding* where Bhaasi incorporates himself into the play, and inventively 'stages' his own entrance and crosses to Ceennan's hut—all accomplished without him actually being there.[10] It is a *coup de théâtre* for Kerala audiences.

Bhaasi also went on to experiment with the adaptation of Sanskrit dramas for the political stage, as in his production of Kalidasa's *Shakuntala* in which he emphasized women's rights and attempted to expose King Dushyanta's problematic attitudes. Others among Bhaasi's dramas have focused specifically on political and/or party/labour union issues. These plays attempt to throw light on the decadence of contemporary leftist politicians, unions, and/or persons in positions of power. *Power House* (*Taapanilayam*, 1990), is a sharp political/social satire focusing on an actual incident of irresponsibility involving the Kerala State Electricity Board. '*Don't Put Your Hand or Head Outside*' is a direct quotation from a sign posted inside all government buses, and becomes a theatrical occasion for Bhaasi to prompt trade union workers to be responsible to their constituents—the masses which constitute the general public.

---

10 Personal interview, June 9, 1993.

Although Bhaasi and KPAC became so synonymous that KPAC was called 'ToopiAC', with Bhaasi considered 'the body and soul of KPAC,'[11] KPAC has also produced plays by other playwrights, such as K.T. Mohammed's *Sutradharan* and *Life Imprisonment*, and three plays authored by Kaniyapuram Ramachandran. And Bhaasi himself took occasional time away from KPAC to pursue other achievements, serving as an MLA twice in 1954 and 1957, and also writing and directing for Malayalam cinema.[12]

Over the forty years of his career in theatre, Tooppil Bhaasi received numerous awards including the Kerala Sahitya Nataka Award, the Central Sangeet Natak Academy Award, and a Kendra Sangeet Nataka Academy Fellowship. *Memories in Hiding* was Bhaasi's last play and an appropriate crowning achievement to his memorable career as a political voice of conscience for the disenfranchized and oppressed during Kerala's years of birth as a new state. Bhaasi adapted *Memories in Hiding* from his 459 page autobiography of the same title, published in 1960 by the National Book Stall in Kottayam. For the stage version, he selected one small, but key incident from the original—the incident at Suranad.

Memories in Hiding received the 1992 Kerala State Government best play award, and KPAC Johnson received the second prize for acting in 1992 for creating the pivotal role of Ceennan in *Memories in Hiding*. Only four days after completing his introduction to *Memories in Hiding* (translated below), Bhaasi died on December 8, 1992. Appropriately, every time *Memories in Hiding* is staged, Bhaasi is still present through his 'absence' as his entrance is staged in this replaying of the Suranad incident.

PHILLIP B. ZARRILLI

---

11 Kaniyapuram Ramachandran interview.

12 Several of his best known dramas, including *You Made Me a Communist* and *Ashwameetam*, were made into films.

PLAYWRIGHT'S INTRODUCTION

Memories in Hiding is my autobiography. It's novel for an individual to dramatize and perform his own autobiography on stage. I don't know if anything quite like it has happened before in India or abroad. Anyway, I decided to try it.

The main element in an autobiography is revealing oneself. When presented on stage, the potential impropriety of self-praise might result. When I began thinking about dramatizing my autobiography, I was afraid it might be self-congratulatory. But as I thought it over I decided my fears were baseless.

The reason is simple—although I talk about myself in my autobiography, it's main focus is on the politics of the period and the radiant sacrifice made by hundreds of persons whom I knew. So I concluded that there was nothing improper in dramatizing [part of my autobiography] as long as I didn't focus on myself, but rather on the political history of the mid-Travancore region during the five years I was in hiding.

Between the first performance of *Memories in Hiding* on 23 August, 1992 until the end of December, I found that my basic premise as well as my conclusion were right. Of these [hundreds of performances] more than forty were in cities like Pune, Bombay, Ahmedabad, and Calcutta. (KPAC had completely booked the play through the 1993 season without a break.) No one who saw the production made a single negative observation as I had feared. Instead, I have received many letters of praise. More important, some scholars of drama have observed that in both my writing and direction I had undergone some changes since *You Made Me a Communist.*

A drama that is presented on the stage should be spectacular. In order to reduce the expression of my 'self,' I remain offstage. Many of the communist leaders whom I mentioned in my original autobiography don't appear onstage. Those characters who do appear are working people–those with financial difficulties, those who sacrifice, those who are unpopular, i.e., 'unpolished' (real) people. Their names have been printed by the ink of my pen. They don't have beautiful physiques nor are they richly ornamented to fit the usual concept of drama. They don't display the erotic sentiment (*srngara*) or other sentiments (*rasas*) to enrich the more ordinary moods (*bhavas*) of the play. Those who live within a system of slavery/oppression don't have those kinds of opportunities. Some characters appear with their actual names. Others are fictional forms of persons living at the time. This was necessary because of the limitations of the theatre.

My main purpose in staging *Memories in Hiding* for a live audience is to portray the decadence of contemporary politics. The majority of politicians see politics as a stepping stone to the highest positions. Though comparatively less so, the communists are not immune to this. This makes me unhappy. There may be rights or wrongs in politics. This can be determined by people from time to time. They can rectify mistakes. Still, for the worker who dedicates his life to a particular political belief, even if it is wrong, his family will always be respected. We must bow before such self-sacrifice.

The political beliefs expressed in *Memories in Hiding* were found to be radically wrong by the Communist Party, and they were eventually rectified. But those who were martyred and suffered while executing these faulty politics are to be respected more than those who rectified them. The political theory of the times known as the 'Calcutta Thesis,' contained not only wrong policies, but right ones too. What was right was the fact that labourers, farmers, and other workers should organize, become conscious of their rights, and through this eradicate feudalism and slavery. What was wrong was that, to achieve this goal, we gave away much more than was needed. The tragic result of these wrong policies affected both the communist leaders and ordinary workers. That's what is shown in this play.

The central event in the play is the Suranad Revolution in which five policemen, including an inspector, were killed. It was wrong. Ten of those involved in the murder case were killed by the police while in jail. Five more, who were released from jail, were also killed through excessive torture. There were twenty-six culprits, including me. The remaining eleven persons still alive are living as martyrs with severe financial difficulties. Who, then, suffered the effects of this misguided policy?

Another noteworthy thing is that the communist leaders of the time were not like the present politicians who deal with faulty policies by sitting in their secure air-conditioned offices, eating *biryani*, and milk pudding, and who tempt ordinary followers to kill and/or to die. The communist leaders themselves were in the battlefield to kill or to die.

The good qualities of a politician are sincerity and sacrifice. The play is intended to help us remember that. As a communist and a literary writer, I humbly undertake this drama as a 'mission' in the context of the contemporary political climate.

There once was a time like this. A time where human lives burned in the 'test fires' of social change. Today, professional politicians should see this. I am satisfied if some among them are prompted to reconsideration.

TOOPPIL BHAASI
[Vallikkunnam, December 4, 1992]

This introduction was published in Malayalam along with the Malayalam script.

Characters

CEENNAN	leader of the Pulayans
TEEVAN	his son, literally 'one who works the pulley pumping water' for irrigation
JANMI	landlord, often called Tamburaan, a Pillai Naayar
NANNU NAAYAR	his bodyguard, a 'wrestler'
PARAMU NAAYAR	friend of Ceenan who is beaten and yoked and later joins the Communist Party revolutionary movement
COMMUNIST WORKERS:	
	Kunnuraaman Parameeswaran Naayar Goopaalapilla (main speaker among the revolutionaries) Raaghavan
POLICE	regular and Reserve
KARAMBI	Ceenan's wife, literally the 'black woman'
NIILI	Teevan's wife, literally from *niila* or the color dark blue associated with Krishna, Kali, or Parvati
PARAMU NAAYAR'S WIFE	
GOOPAALAPILLA'S WIFE	
YOUNG WOMAN	
GOONDA	rowdy in landlord's pay
STAGE MANAGER	
ACTRESS IN THE COMPANY	
Offstage voices:	Tooppil Bhaasi, Police Inspector

PROLOGUE (*NANDI*)[1]

The Stage Manager enters and bows to the audience.

STAGE MANAGER. Respected audience members, I am the Stage Manager. Since this is a special drama, a prologue is necessary to explain the historical background of this drama. We will perform Tooppil Bhaasi's autobiographical drama, *Memories in Hiding*. It is unusual for an individual to dramatize and direct his own autobiography. First, for this writer his autobiography is less concerned with personal than with social affairs. In the original text of 459 pages are described hundreds of people's actual (and not fictional) stories which occurred in one historical period. Within the limitations of a two-and-a-half hour theatre performance, it's only possible to perform the most essential points of the stories of one group of characters. The Suranad Revolution is the essence of *Memories in Hiding*.

The Communist Party led that revolution. Naturally, there were mistakes in the Party's policies, but they were more right than wrong. At that time the bad effects of these misguided policies were experienced by both the followers and the leaders—including comrades E.M.S. [Namboodiripad], Achutha Menon, K. C. George, as well as other party workers. Yes, this is the history of the end of feudalism and slavery. The historical incident that happened forty-five years ago we are recreating for you here today. The characters in this play are the ordinary people who were trampled underfoot, suffered, and died in slavery. These characters are not 'glamorous.' Since they are bearing the burden of slavery's yoke, it's impossible for them to 'dally in love play.'[2] The drama we are performing today has a special purpose. It is a warning against allowing contemporary political decadence. Political work must be a radiant sacrifice. No

---

1 The *nandi* is a traditional prologue for Sanskrit dramas. This is the only one of Bhaasi's plays which uses this device. The prologue typically begins with the appearance of the Stage Manager, who calls forth a member of the acting company, often a female, to whom he puts questions which suggest what follows in the drama proper. Implicit in its use here is a subtle parody of the conventions of Sanskrit drama.

2 Bhaasi uses the English word, 'glamour,' which is freely associated with popular romantic films and/or Parsi-type musical dramas. The Malayalam term we translate as 'dally in love play' is *srngarikuka*, from the Sanskrit *srngara* or the erotic sentiment typical in Sanskrit dramas and prevalent in traditional dance and dance-drama genres like Kerala's *kathakali*.

one should use politics as a stepping stone to reach a position of power.[3] This play will help you remember those selfless, little known, dedicated politicians. (*Looking toward the green room*) Will one of the actresses please come forward to pay respects to the audience.

An actress enters, pays respects to the audience.

STAGE MANAGER. What did the director say were the important things to remember about this drama?

ACTRESS. Yes. On this stage itself, we will enact the original text, (*gesturing to the stage and the audience*) respected audience.

STAGE MANAGER. On the stage, we will perform the original version without alterations so that you the audience, we the actors, and the drama itself will be completely joined together in sharing a common experience.[4]

ACTRESS. But is it possible for us to share the same experience when the audience consists of different persons, those with different political points of view, as well as critics?

STAGE MANAGER. It should be possible. If we activate the audience's memories, their minds will be filled with a vision (of the past).

ACTRESS. Although the writer and director is not with us to act, I wish he were with us as a major character.

STAGE MANAGER. That's not necessary. This is not only his experience in hiding; thousands throughout the country had the same experience or worse, and in many other places. So, it's not necessary to reduce this historical context to the presence of our writer alone. We have introduced all the necessary background in this prologue.

Let us begin our performance of *Memories in Hiding* with a song about the slavery and feudalism that existed in our beautiful villages a half-century ago. Sing! (*Looking offstage*) Chorus and actors, join us in singing the prologue to this drama.

Offstage, background music is heard, as well as a temple bell and conch. The actors and actresses from offstage join the stage manager and actress in singing.

SONG. [*The song at the end of the prologue conveys the mood of a village at*

---

3 Strongly implied here is a criticism of current leadership in leftist political circles which has used politics to gain power both within particular parties as well as when in positions of leadership in the state government.

4 Implicit in Bhaasi's use of *tanmayiibhaviikumboo Raanu*, or the experience of 'merging or joining together' is a criticism of the recent espousal among leftist dramatists and theatre workers in Kerala of an explicitly Brechtian definition of dramatic structure and aesthetic experience. Bhaasi here reasserts the need for a drama of 'identification.'

that time, painting a poetic picture of the place.]

(Refrain) The celestial Ganga waves
Tremulous stars reach the paddy fields.
Holding the silver lamp in her hand,
Dawn arrives at the doorway to the earth.

(*When the refrain ends, in the Western sky the red light of sunset.*)

Poorkali Bhagavati appeared wearing her crown.[5]
Wearing her bangles
[the time for] Mudiyeettu has come.[6]
Banyan leaves sang rhythmically.
The immortal divine singers added the *tilana*.[7]

[refrain]

In the wind, the palm leaves provide the *sruti*.[8]
Women onlookers will come to murmur stories.
The sound of the bamboo spilled.
The smell of the civet cat draws near.

[refrain]

The Stage Manager and Actress bow to the audience as they step backward and exit.

5 Poorkali Bhagavati is the village deity of the Suranad area where the action of the play takes place. Bhagavati is a fierce form of the goddess, and is the deity of war. Poorkali is her specific local form in this village.
6 Mudiyeettu is a local form of ritual possession drama in which the defeat of the demon Darikan by the goddess Kali (or Bhadrakali) is enacted in all-night performances.
7 The *tilana* is a vocal genre in music or dance concert which features drum syllables as text.
8 The *sruti* is the pitch, interval, or intonation.

ACT ONE

Scene 1

Very large paddy field. Partially planted, and partially unplanted. To the east the rising sun's red rays gradually dim. Dim light before the rising of the sun. The sound of morning birds. In the distance somewhere, a cow's lowing. The natural beauty of the village is evoked. Led by the 'one who takes precise steps' [a reference to the leader of the wheel pumpers who literally stands in place as he operates the wheel pump by stepping] as he sings and sets a rhythm, each verse is repeated by the other pumpers. On a twelve platform wheel, five workers are working. On each side of and below the leader two others are stepping.

taa–tii–too–taatii–too
takataka, takataka, tiiyoo–

Humming again. In this way the combination of work and art continues. In between, a change of rhythm.

Loafer–*ese*
push harder–*ese*
bullocks come–*ese*
water dried up–*ese*
tamburaan will come–*ese*
gruel will come–*ese*
roots and stems–*ese*.

Improvise other words to the song. All verses should reflect their intense dislike of the janmi system in a mocking tone.

The head Pulayan enters with a spade on his shoulders. He is almost sixty years old. He wears a towel, muddy with dirt. When working mud was smeared all over his body. He sits on the paddy field's ridge path, removes his hat and prepares paan to chew. The morning star's light shines on his body. Ceennan looks in the direction of the wheel pullers offstage. His expression is that of one who controls everything.

CEENNAN. Teevaa? (*Teevan answers, off*).

CEENNAN. Who is the lead stepper on the wheel? Is it Caattan?

TEEVAN (*off*). Yes.

CEENNAN. Within half an hour the water should be gone. The bullocks are coming for ploughing. (*Stands and comes forward looking off left, he calls. In the distance a woman calls back.)*

CEENNAN. The sun has risen one yoke, and the women paddy field workers haven't come yet. (*Again he calls. Two women call back, and one woman calls, 'We're coming.'*)

CEENNAN (*angrily*). Don't come! If work doesn't begin at the right time, the landlord will push me into the muddy field. I am the head Pulayan. Tamburaan will ask me. (*The women workers cross upstage on the ridge path, some wearing towels on their heads, some covered with mats to avoid the cold.*)

CEENNAN. Impure women shouldn't come to plant.[9] They should go to the nursery plot to pluck and clean the baby plants.

One Pulayan woman, Ceennan's wife, Karambi, enters. She dislikes Ceennan's comment. She is about fifty years old. Some women are walking behind her. The woman in front of her exits. The others wait behind.

KARAMBI. So, are you teaching women's manners and behaviour?

CEENNAN. Hey! What I said didn't involve you. Since you're so old you're not impure. I only meant this for the younger women.

KARAMBI. Look! Impure women bathe in a flowing stream before coming to work, and those having their period won't even come!

CEENNAN (*as if lecturing her*). Hey! I want to explain what I just said. Last year a few days after the young rice was planted, the entire crop was eaten by worms. Do you know why? (*secretly whispering to her*). One impure woman came to plant. I found out why (*looking around, very softly*). It was the Tamburaan himself!

KARAMBI (*angrily*). If the landlord did it, then *all* the plants *should* be worm eaten!

CEENNAN (*suddenly comes forward angrily*). I'll give you a beating.

KARAMBI. Didn't the landlord do something immoral?

CEENNAN. If there's a crop failure, it'll be my fault. As the head Pulayan it's my duty to fill the landlord's granary.

KARAMBI. Well, fill it up! I'm not impure. (*Scowling unpleasantly she leaves by the ridge path. The others exit with her.*)

CEENNAN (*replying to Karambi*) That's only because I'm an old man! (*All*

---

9 This traditional notion of impurity could be caused either by a women in menses or one who had engaged in sex the night before. Either is understood to cause disease to the rice plants.

exit giggling, except Karambi. The wheel pullers' song is heard. Looking off he sees someone and calls) Teeva, the women coming should plant the Kannimel plots. Are there enough?

TEEVAN'S VOICE. Yes!

CEENNAN. The women coming from the west are planting a seven *para* block of paddy. Plant a few closer together.

The sound of the bullock's bell to the right. Someone drives the bullocks with a stick. Ceennan looks off in that direction.

CEENNAN. Paramu Naayar Tamburaan, please stop!

The sound of the bullocks stops. When the bullocks stop the sound of the bells also stops.

CEENNAN. Since you were late with the bullocks from the landlord's house, I hired a pair of daily workers to plough and plane the field. After they finish ploughing the middle fields, use the bullocks to plane. Then tie them there.

The sound of the bullocks has moved away. The wheel song stops.

CEENNAN (*looking off right and shouting*) Hurry up and finish ploughing the middle block and go on to the lower block! The wheel pullers are finished and the lower block is ready.

After tying the bullocks, the bullock driver Paramu Naayar enters. He is a young man wearing a T-shirt, coloured dhoti,[10] *and a towel wrapped around his head. He holds a long stick.*

CEENNAN (*to Paramu Naayar*). Why are you late?

PARAMU NAAYAR (*ill-tempered*). At four o'clock this morning I went to the landlord's bungalow and starting grinding the horse gram until daybreak. When I was going to feed it to the bullocks, the landlord came and watched me. He abused me for not grinding it the right way and then wanted me to grind it all over again! Finally I fed the bullocks and gave them a rub-down.

CEENNAN (*happily*). Tamburaan himself went to the Maman Market and bought that bullock. (*The clanging sound of the bullocks' bells are heard.*)

PARAMU NAAYAR. He sympathizes with animals, but not with the

---

10 A cloth wrapped around the waist. Colored dhotis are also called lungis and were usually worn by labourers, field workers, and servants. They contrast with the white lower and upper cloths worn by higher castes and landholders whom they serve and/or for whom they labour.

labourers who turn their blood into water. (*He sits on the path ridge.*)

CEENNAN. Even though Tamburaan beats and abuses us as his slaves, he still loves us.[11]

PARAMU NAAYAR (*with subtle sarcasm*). Oh yes, yes! The day Ceennan Pulayan was beaten, he used to get five measures of rice and one cup of oil.[12]

CEENNAN (*smiling*). It's an age-old custom.

PARAMU NAAYAR. Naayar and Ezhava workers don't get anything when they are beaten.[13]

CEENNAN (*proudly*). We've always been slaves! But I never take my additional wages to my hut.[14] Instead, I give it to the toddy shop to cure my body pains.[15] For five measures of rice, I get five coconut shells of toddy!

PARAMU NAAYAR. Are they still giving toddy in shells?

CEENNAN. There are cups, but they are for Tamburaans. Pulayas and Parayas can't use them.[16] If Paramu Naayar Tamburaan goes, you'll get your toddy in a cup.

PARAMU NAAYAR (*meaningfully*). It's likely that Ceennan Pulayan's toddy

---

11 The Malayalam word *adiyan* may be translated as 'slave', 'servant', or even tenant. It implies a relationship in servitude/service to someone of higher and more powerful status. The particular inflection given when translating *adiyan* depends upon our reading of the particular relationship and the attitude of the *adiyan* toward the service relationship. Pulayans and other lower castes were tenant-labourers who in effect were considered the 'property' of the landlords and therefore functioned almost like slaves. Other higher castes who served landholders more as servants, would not have been considered 'property' totally at the disposal of the landlord. These gradations are a matter of degree as well as kind.

Since at this point in the play Ceennan happily accepts his position of servitude and does not question it, he assumes that he is completely servile to the Tamburaan he serves, i.e., he functions as his 'slave' whom the landlord has the 'right' to beat. The landlord's attitude toward Niili also assumes that as a Pulayan woman she is his 'property' to have if and when he desires her.

12 Traditionally when the lowest castes in service to a landlord were beaten, they were given additional provisions for the beating they had received.

13 Castes higher than Pulayans had a status more as servants than as slaves, i.e., they were not considered the 'property' of those whom they served, and so when beaten they would not be given additional provisions.

14 Specific types of houses have specific names, each of which has a traditional caste/class affiliation in Malayalam. Therefore, we have translated *maatam*, the term for a thatched mud-floor low-caste house in which labourers would live as 'hut.' We have used the English 'bungalow' for the landlord's house to indicate its grandness.

15 Toddy is fermented coconut milk. An indigenous intoxicant.

16 Pulayas and Parayas were traditionally considered the lowest among the 'polluting' Hindu castes. See Appendix I for a discussion on the traditional Kerala caste hierarchy which is essential for understanding the class and caste issues raised in the play.

drinking is going to stop.

CEENNAN. When I die even my funeral *puja* will be performed with a jar of toddy![17]

PARAMU NAAYAR. What I mean is, you'll no longer drink toddy with the wages you get for taking a beating. Beatings by landlords are being stopped.

CEENNAN (*unbelievingly*). Where?

PARAMU NAAYAR. In the north . . . in Kuttanad . . . in Vaikom . . . in Edappalli. Don't you know what happened in Ennakkatte?

CEENNAN (*seriously*). I heard about that. The landlord of the village sent his people to forcefully evict Kanjira Vila Kutty Pulayan from his hut. With the help of tenants from other castes, the Pulayas stopped them. That Tamburaan got the police to help. Then the police arrested the Pulayas and others, and chained them together. They were forced to walk through the streets in their chains, as if they were animals being taken to the butcher.

PARAMU NAAYAR (*indignantly, as if he sees the horrible incident before him. His facial expression changes.*) The policeman thrust their lathis[18] directly into the workers' backs, and then beat them with the barrels of their guns. They kicked those who fell down with the help of the goondas. Some of those who were tortured were bleeding. The workers' wives and children were following them, openly crying. All the villagers who gathered there stood aside fearfully along the road.

While hearing Paramu Naayar's description, Ceennan is frozen in place in a state of shock, as if he too sees everything in front of him. A few moments later he takes a long breath and regains his normal state.

CEENNAN. Well, they should suffer for rebelling against their Tamburaans.

PARAMU NAAYAR (*angrily*). They may have suffered, but they stopped their landlords from beating them! If they want to beat them again, they'll have to get the police to help them.

CEENNAN. The police will obey whatever the Tamburaans say. So why should the Tamburaans go to the trouble of beating them and risk becoming impure?[19] (*As if telling a secret to Paramu Naayar*) I heard

---

17 *Puja* is the most typical form of worship for popular Hindu deities. Offerings pleasing to each deity are given daily such as flame (pleasing to sight), incense (pleasing to smell), drumming or music (pleasing to sound), and a wide variety of foods (for taste).
18 *Lathis* are solid cane sticks used as baton-weapons by the police.
19 A reference to the impurity caused when a higher caste person touches or is touched by someone of a lower caste. As explained in Appendix I, until the twentieth century, Kerala

that Ennakkatte Tamburaan's sons cooked up the plot and convinced the Pulayas and others to participate.[20] The oldest son—his name is Sankara Narayanan Nambi—was helped by Puthupalli Raaghavan. They are communists hiding from the police. They were the ones who caused all this trouble by hiding in Kanjira Vila Kutty's hut. (*Looking off left*) Our grand Tamburaan is coming!

Paramu Naayar looks to the left, and with respect takes the towel from his head.

CEENNAN. Yoke the bullocks. Let's plane the centre block. (*Paramu Naayar goes to the bullocks. Ceennan looks left, in the direction of the landlord, respectfully, and turns to the right*). Why don't you start planting. (*Calling out*) Teeva! Spread out that bunch of baby plants.

The sound of the bullocks moving. From the left the landlord enters, walking along the ridge path. He is wearing a white dhoti and a long, light white cotton shirt. Someone is walking behind him as if he is his manager and bodyguard. He holds a box for paan. His name is Nannu Naayar. He walks like a wrestler, flexing his chest muscles. He coughs continuously. Ceennan looks at the landlord and steps aside respectfully.

JANMI (*to Ceennan*). Why are you so late starting the planting?

CEENNAN. Tamburaan, from early this morning I started calling and crowing.

NANNU NAAYAR. So, instead of the cock, Ceennan is crowing everyone awake!

CEENNAN. I have to crow since I'm the head Pulayan. But I am not a cock.[21]

Nannu Naayar looks at the landlord as if there was something more implied in what he said. Then he looks at Ceennan.

NANNU NAAYAR. Did you hear this Pulaya's insult! (*Implying that Ceennan is lying. He looks at the landlord. His look suggests that Ceennan was calling the landlord himself a 'cock'.*)

---

possessed some of the most rigid distance pollution rules in India.

20 Some of the inspiration and leadership within the early communist movement was given by the sons of well-to-do and/or high-caste landholders.

21 The comic by-play here is around the not-so-sûbtle implications of the word 'cock', i.e., if a man is a 'cock' he conquers all the hens in the yard. Even though Ceennan himself, in his response to Nannu Naayar's taunt, simply answers his question literally and is not suggesting anything more, the humour lies in the fact that Nannu Naayar reads into Ceennan's answer an implication that this low-caste Pulayan may be insulting the landlord. The humour is furthered by the fact that landlords like this one were 'cocks' of their roosts, and often actually took the hens of their choice from among their low-caste tenants.

CEENNAN. I would never say anything insulting.

NANNU NAAYAR. You said that you are not a cock, didn't you? You implied that someone else here is a cock. (*He looks at the landlord as if Ceennan meant that he was the cock.*) You weren't referring to me. So far, no one has ever called me a wild cock. So, who exactly did you mean? (*Glances at the landlord.*)

JANMI. So, Pulayas are becoming proud!

NANNU NAAYAR. Of course, but they shouldn't be *this* proud. We can ignore what others say, but when your own tenant says this directly to your face? (*Coughs.*)

CEENNAN (*innocently*). What's wrong with what I said, Tamburaan?

NANNU NAAYAR (*to the landlord*). He wants to repeat his insult!

JANMI. Hey! Ceennaa, you are taking the Kettukatta and Allakkida[22] intended for the head Pulayan.

CEENNAN. Yes.

JANMI. Then why didn't you bring the workers early this morning?

CEENNAN. Yesterday evening itself I began pulling the twelve-needled water wheel. By very early this morning we had pumped out all the water from the down side blocks of paddy and I started calling all the workers to wake up, even before the cock-crows.

NANNU NAAYAR (*to the landlord*). Listen! He's starting in with that cock story again! Pulayans, Kuravans, and Parayans are really becoming arrogant!

CEENNAN. I'm not arrogant, Tamburaan.

JANMI. You know what your son, Teevan, said to my wife yesterday when he came to eat? He didn't want his rice gruel served from the cooking pot! He wanted it on a 'leaf'!!![23]

NANNU NAAYAR (*surprised*). Ayyooo![24] Did he say that! Why, when he sits down to eat from a leaf, he expects your wife to bend down in front of him to serve him the gruel. (*He mimes her bending over, exposing her breasts to him, and reacting.*)

---

22 That is, you are enjoying the privileges of being the head Pulayan and taking these special bundles of rice.

23 Taking food from the pot itself means that someone is in an abject position of servitude and is taking only what is left over after everyone else is done eating. To be 'served' on a 'leaf' (a traditional 'plate' of banana leaf) would mean that one expects to be treated as an equal.

24 The most common colloquial expression used to express a variety of responses.

JANMI (*angrily*). From now on I'll give him his gruel in the same pot from which I feed my dog!

NANNU NAAYAR. Don't do that! Don't give Teevan gruel from the same pot in which you feed Kaisar meat and rice! Kaisar won't eat meat and rice from a pot used by a Pulayan! Even though he's a dog, he's an aristocrat! It's your dog!

CEENNAN. I wouldn't object like Teevan did. I used to eat in the copper vessel that you used to feed the animals. At your house, I have never once in my life eaten fresh rice gruel. The rice gruel I get is always partially eaten by the crows, Tamburaan.

NANNU NAAYAR. What do you mean? Are you trying to prove that when the gruel is prepared, we clap and call the Bali crows to eat it before we give it to you?[25]

CEENNAN. When Tamburaan's wife comes out of the kitchen with the rice gruel, I always step back a few steps to keep myself away from her. She leaves it outside for me and returns. Only after she's back in the kitchen do I go near the food. The crows know this routine, and they come and eat some of the food before I can get to it.

JANMI (*mockingly*). I shall do one thing. From today onward, I'll serve you food inside my own house with all formalities. (*He exits to oversee the work.*)

NANNU NAAYAR (*laughing as if this is a joke*). Yes, Pulayan. For everything there are appropriate customs and manners. You know that I am a Naayar?

CEENNAN. Yes!

NANNU NAAYAR (*pointing to the landlord*). I'm his 'bodyguard' (*coughs*).[26]

CEENNAN (*failing to understand the English word*). Who?

NANNU NAAYAR. 'Bodyguard'. I was a wrestler.[27] The Tamburaan was my patron and he made all preparations for my wrestling with Electric Mytheen! He was patronized by Kumballathu Sanku Pillai! When the wrestling match would reach its peak of intensity, there was a special trick move that was applied. Not by me, but by Electric.

---

25 This is a reference to a series of offerings (*puja*) for the salvation of a soul. After death, the priest (*pujari*), prepares rice which is given as an offering to the crows. He calls the crows by clapping his hands. If the crows come it is a positive sign that the soul is at peace.
26 'Bodyguard' is in English throughout.
27 Wrestling was a very important traditional sport in India. Wrestlers were often patronized by rulers who had their own stables of competition wrestlers. On Indian wrestling, see Joseph P. Alter, *The Wrestler's Body: Identity and Ideology in North India* (Berkeley: University of California Press, 1992).

(*Coughing.*) No, no, not by Electric, but by me. Since that cough was never cured, I became his bodyguard.

Some jealously call me 'Rowdy'. Even a person like me never eats inside his bungalow. I always take my meals sitting in the kitchen veranda. And I myself wash the copper dish I eat from, and put it upside down. I clean and purify the place. Do you know why? (*The landlord enters*).

CEENNAN. There must be some reason.

NANNU NAAYAR. Yes. There is a reason. Although I'm a Naayar, I'm a Thoruvakkaran Naayar. Tamburaan belongs to the noble line of Pillais!

A shout in the distance.

CEENNAN (*looking to the distance*). The bullocks are yoked. (*Crossing toward the landlord*) I ought to go plane the field. No one can do it as well as I can. (*He exits to the right with his spade on his shoulder.*)

The landlord opens his palm to Nannu Naayar—indicating that he wants paan. Nannu Naayar opens the paan box and gives some to the landlord. They continue talking.

NANNU NAAYAR. Pulayas, Parayas, and all the others must be controlled. Don't you know what happened in Ennakkatte?

JANMI (*smiling*). Pulayans and others were severely beaten and kicked by the police and the village Tamburaan's men as if they were making a chutney!

Shouting intended to speed up the ploughing of the bullocks is heard. It is a lengthy and musical series of shouts. The landlord and Nannu Naayar look off in that direction and enjoy watching the bullocks ploughing. As the bullocks plough in circles, their eyes follow their movements.

NANNU NAAYAR (*after a short pause, continuing their conversation*). There have been some disturbances in areas like Vallikkunnath. The Pillai of Kadakal called his *chotti* servant maid, 'Chokkuzhiyatti'.[28] When her husband heard this he snapped back as if slapping him on the face, 'Her name is Kunnipenne. Call her by her name!' (*He gives him tobacco.*)

JANMI (*laughing sarcastically*). *Chotti* should be called a lord-ess (*spitting*).

NANNU NAAYAR. As if the women of Kambisserry Channar's and

---

28 A sexually suggestive pet name, parodying high caste women.

Alummoottil Channar's are called that—all Chovans want their women to be called Channatti.

JANMI. Didn't brother Kadakkal do anything against the one who spoke out?

NANNU NAAYAR. He is a communist! His name is something like Kunjiraman.

Sounds of the bullocks running is frequently heard.

NANNU NAAYAR. Some upstart youths from respectable families are supporting him. One is a young man from Tooppil.[29]

JANMI. Bhaasi! Along with Kambisserry Channar's son, Karunakaran, a Potti teacher of Vallikkunnam school, they were Congressmen.

NANNU NAAYAR. At that time they were supporters of C.P.[30]

JANMI (*as if remembering*). Don't say things like that now. Now we're all Congress.

NANNU NAAYAR. Bhaasi is also hiding from the police. If he's caught, he'll be treated like the Pulayas of Ennakkatte.

JANMI. He'll eventually be caught. Our police aren't too bad.

A planter's song is heard from a distance. Nannu Naayar looks in that direction.

NANNU NAAYAR. Planting has begun in the Kannimmel block.

The landlord looks in that direction and exits to the right, followed by Nannu Naayar. The lights fade.

Scene 2

As the lights come up, there is a spectacular scene of a paddy field. A planter's song is heard. The voices become louder and louder. The landlord and Nannu Naayar enter from the left. From the right a group of women planters, moving backwards, sing while planting rice in the field. As they enter moving backwards while planting, their backsides are seen first.

---

29 The first of a series of references to Tooppil Bhaasi, the playwright and director. Tooppil is Bhaasi's family name. Bhaasi's shadow presence as a communist in hiding becomes a simultaneously serious as well as comic leitmotif throughout the play.

30 Sir C. P. Ramaswami Iyer, Divan of Travancore. As Divan he proposed that communists should be treated like stray dogs and killed on sight. In the 1930's this Tamil Brahman was severely beaten by communists who attempted to murder him. Subsequent to the beatings he left Travancore to live in Tamil Nadu.

PLANTERS' SONG:

(Refrain) Tintaaree-tintaaree-
tintaaree-taka tintaaree
tintaaree-tintaaree
tintaaree-taka tintaaree.

With mylanchi polished hands[31]
planting women
planted planted
moving backward.

(Refrain)

When the auspicious time has come
go into the Karakkandam field.
When the Karakkandam is finished
[Let's] drink Karikkadi water.[32]

(Refrain)

While sitting on the branch of a
sweet mango tree
Teevan is playing his flute.
In the muddy field, looking at [him]
[is] Niili, the oily black-colored girl.

(Refrain)

Patiently waiting, playful Kannan[33]
Caught river fish on his hook.
A lovely lord, holding a round-shaped umbrella
comes wobbling with his huge stomach.

(Refrain)

The refrain is sung by the group. It is led by a planter. During the planting song, the sounds from planing the fields are heard. The landlord enjoys watching the backsides of the women as they plant. As the planters move backwards from the center of the stage, the landlord and his assistant walk ahead and then turn back and watch the front of the planters. Whenever one young woman, Niili, stands up and wipes her foreheard, the landlord looks at her excitedly and whispers something to Nannu Naayar, who also replies with a whisper. The

31 Mylanchi is used by women to create orange-colored designs on their hands and feet.
32 A herbal water.
33 Krishna

women move backward and exit on the opposite side of the stage. The song is heard from a distance.

JANMI. Who is that woman, Nannu Naayar?

NANNU NAAYAR. She's the wife of Ceennan's son.

JANMI. I haven't seen her before.

NANNU NAAYAR. She came here last month after their marriage. Didn't they bring her to your house to 'take' her?[34]

JANMI. No.

NANNU NAAYAR. Certainly she can't be brought without being 'taken'. They have to bring something like pounded rice with them, and that is a bit expensive. That's why they're delaying it. Certainly she won't not be taken since whenever one of them is taken they're supposed to get a new dhoti and five measures of rice.

JANMI. Look, Nannu Naayar, this evening I'll go to the granary. (*Smiling meaningfully*) Follow what I mean?

NANNU NAAYAR (*smiling*). Haven't I been with you yesterday and today? What you see in your mind, I see in the sky!

The sounds of the bullocks from the ploughing fields. The landlord and Nannu Naayar walk in that direction along the ridge path as they exit. The lights fade out.

Scene 3

Another side of the paddy fields. The landlord and Nannu Naayar enter from the left. From the paddy ridge they step down onto a grassy plain and look at the planing of the field. From the look on their faces, it is evident that the bullocks are running.

JANMI. The Myla bullock is one step ahead.

NANNU NAAYAR. The spotted bullock is walking at almost the same pace. How many teeth does it have?

JANMI. It has all its teeth. But the other one only has four. The spotted bullock should be exchanged.

NANNU NAAYAR. To find a suitable mate for the Myla bullock, we will

---

34 The verb here is *kutivekka* which means 'to take a wife' or to settle her in her house after marriage. It is clearly implied that the Landlord has the right to 'take her' or settle her himself.

have to go to Kannatt Market. Good pairs are available at the Oochirakali festival.[35]

JANMI. We can go look in Oomallur. After this planting season, the bullocks should be given Thanuppu medicine prepared from two black chickens ground in Ariyar and cumin seed.[36]

NANNU NAAYAR. Oh, I have a 'chicken' for you. Not a cock, but a hen! (*Smiles.*)

JANMI. We should take them to the Mughatala bullock race.

NANNU NAAYAR. When we take them, we'll give them Veeppu oil for energy. It can only be given two weeks after the Thanuppu medicine has been taken. It would be grand to travel to Mughatala in a decorated cart drawn by the ornamented bullocks with small bells on their necks and pointed bronze caps on the tips of their horns.

A beating sound is heard from the side where the planing is taking place. The landlord is flushed with anger.

JANMI (*shouting*). Stop the bullocks!

NANNU NAAYAR (*more loudly*). Stop the bullocks!

JANMI. Chi, rascal! I said stop the bullocks!!!

The sound of the bullocks stopping.

JANMI (*shouting angrily*). Paramu and Ceennan, come here!!

NANNU NAAYAR. Oh! He has beaten your bullock![37] (*The landlord angrily glares at him.*) Your Myla bullock has been beaten on its back! (*The landlord stands still, and becomes even more angry.*) You yourself went to the market and specially selected that bullock. It's so beautiful it should only be fondled and petted, not beaten.

Paramu Naayar and Ceennan enter from the right. Their clothes and bodies are smeared with mud. Paramu Naayar holds a stick.

JANMI (*to Paramu Naayar*). Have you beaten my bullock?

PARAMU NAAYAR. I gave him a light tap when he failed to turn around at the end of the field.

NANNU NAAYAR (*surprised*). Was that a 'light tap'? Its back might have been broken!

---

35 Oochirakali is a village in the mid-Travancore region noted for its large monsoon temple festival. Along with the festival a major animal market is set up for the buying, selling, and trading of bullocks, cows, etc.

36 A traditional Ayurvedic medical preparation.

37 For many landlords their lead bullock was often considered their special 'pet' animal in whom they took great pride and for whom they had great affection.

The landlord angrily grabs the stick from Paramu Naayar and starts beating him. When he tries to move away, the landlord kicks him down and continues beating him mercilessly.

CEENNAN (*sorrowfully*). He didn't mean to hurt it! He only hit it when it didn't turn around.

JANMI. So you're taking his side! (*Crosses to him and begins to beat him mercilessly too.*)

CEENNAN. Oh, Tamburaan, I didn't do anything wrong!

The landlord continues to beat him. The women planters enter from the left. When they see what's happening they feel sorry for Ceennan, but are afraid for themselves.

JANMI (*stops beating Ceennan and looks to the right, shouting*). Teeva! Take the yoke off the bullocks and bring it here! (*After a pause*) What's taking you so long? Bring it here right now or you'll be next!!!

CEENNAN (*painfully touching where he was beaten*). Tamburaan Lord, you can beat or kick me since I'm your tenant. But you shouldn't have beaten that Naayar boy. It's the duty of the ploughman to teach ploughing to a bullock.

JANMI. So, are you trying to teach me? (*Continues beating him. Ceennan's wife, Karambi, and the other women begin to cry loudly. Turning to the women*) Go and get back to work!

NANNU NAAYAR (*to the women*). What do you want to see here? Go and get back to work! (*He crosses toward them. Continuing to cry, they all move back fearfully.*)

With a sorrowful expression on his face, Teevan enters with the yoke.

JANMI. Yoke together your father and his Naayar boy. Instead of bullocks, they can do the ploughing! (*Teevan stands still.*) Chi! Won't you obey my orders!

CEENNAN. Dear son, don't disobey Tamburaan. (*He bends down like a bullock to bear the yoke. Teevan places one end of the yoke on his neck. Nannu Naayar pulls Paramu Naayar from the floor and forcefully bends him down to place the other end of the yoke on his neck. The women cry.*)

JANMI. Yoke them tightly and take them to the muddy field. I won't leave until I've seen their ploughing!

He climbs up onto the paddy ridge and exits to the right. Nannu Naayar follows him. Teevan finishes yoking his father and Paramu Naayar. The loud wailing of the women is heard as the lights fade to black.

ACT TWO

Scene 1

A place where tenant farmers live. A small hut on the side of the paddy fields. It is Ceennan's hut. A broken bench is kept outside. It is late evening. The light of a kerosene lamp comes from the hut. The paddy fields are slightly visible in the fading light of the setting sun. Sounds from other nearby huts are heard. There are also sounds of chickens being caught and put in a cage. An infant is crying. Its mother begins to sing a lullaby. The child stops crying. The shadow of a young woman labourer appears.

YOUNG WOMAN (*calling*). Auntie Karambi?

KARAMBI (*from the hut*). Yeh? (*She comes out with a kerosene lamp. In the lamplight, the scene and the outline of the young woman are clear.*)

YOUNG WOMAN. Can you lend me five green peppers?

KARAMBI (*uneasily*). No, my dear.

YOUNG WOMAN. When the planting was over, Velutha and I went to fish in the brook. We caught a few, but don't have any peppers to cook it with.

KARAMBI. The peppers we had we cooked with the tapioca.[38]
I saw Sankaran's wife, Koravan—she's going to the shop to buy peppers and salt. Ask her for some.

YOUNG WOMAN (*looking around*). It's getting dark.

KARAMBI. The moon is about to come out.

The Young Woman exits. Karambi puts the lamp on the bench and turns to go back inside. From the left a Kakkarissi song is heard.[39] She looks in the direction of the song. She becomes angry when she realizes that it's Ceennan who is singing. Suddenly, she goes inside the hut. From the

---

38 Tapioca, and the small fish caught in local brooks are typical food of the poor and lower castes.

39 *Kakkarissi natakam* is a traditional form of folk drama popular in the central and southern Travancore region of Kerala. In central Travancore where the play is set, it is performed by low caste Panars and Kammalars. The play combines music, dance, and acting. The character known as *Sundara Kaakkaan* enters and commences a dialogue with the audience. Then he calls the women and the play begins. Other characters include a hunter (Vedan), women, Tampuraan, Kuravan, forest tiger and Kurathi. The three to five hour performance takes place at night. Its many sub-plots make fun of the local 'big wigs.' (*Folk Arts Directory*, 1978, 48-9).

left Ceennan enters, imitating the steps and movements of the Kakkan who performs in the folk drama. The rice he received as his daily wage is covered in his towel and hangs as a bundle from the end of a long stick on his shoulder.

CEENNAN (*Singing*)[40]

Takataka teyyattaaroo-teyyattaaroo
Kattaanam Nalluttadeesam–Oh, Tamburaan!
I am the idiot who rules Kattachira.
Takataka teyyattaaroo-teyyattaaroo
I am the idiot who rules Kattachira.
Anappadi Chunakara and good Vettkkott,
and Maraman and Ayirur and Thiruvayiur.
Kattanam Nalluttadeesam–Oh, Tamburaan!
I am the idiot who rules Kattachira.

He jumps and dances outside, and then looks into the hut.

Hey! Kakkathis![41]
(*To himself*) Oh, I only have one Kakkathi!!!
Yeh, an *old* Kakkathi.

KARAMBI (*coming out of the hut indignantly*). You're going beyond your limit, old man!! (*Crossing to him*) I'm not a Kakkathi. I'm a Pulaki!![42]

CEENNAN (*he takes the rice bundle from his stick and puts the stick on her neck, leaping and dancing up and down*). You jump and play, Kakkathi! Old Kakkathi

Taka, taka, tittoom, teyyoom
taka, taka, tiittoom, teyyoom.

Karambi pushes the stick away and moves back.

KARAMBI. So, the Old Pulayan has come home after drinking his toddy!

CEENNAN. I drank toddy to cure my body pains. But I haven't taken a single grain from my wages (*showing the bundle*). Here's my wages!

KARAMBI. If you hurt so much, stop your jumping around and dancing! Go and lie down!

CEENNAN. I'm not going to lie down. But she's going to bed me even before it gets dark!!

---

40 A Pulayan does not normally perform Kakkarissi, but in his drunken state he starts performing it. In this state he has 'become' a Kakkan—a member of an even lower caste.
The following version of a Kakkarissi song is made up of the syllables of the rhythmic steps, and nonsensical phrases, all combined in Ceennan's drunken imitation of the Kakkan performer.

41 Women of the caste that performs Kakkarissi.

42 A Pulayan woman.

KARAMBI (*warning him*). Pulayan has to go to work tomorrow. I say go and lie down!

CEENNAN (*angrily pointing with his stick*). I'll beat you! (*Karambi stands still and pays no attention to his threat. Ceennan also stands still pointing with his stick. Given his state of intoxication, he suddenly starts crying. Karambi continues to stand there unaffected by his sobbing. When he has controlled his crying*) Yeh, Karambi?

.KARAMBI (*lovingly*). Yeh?

CEENNAN (*standing with his stick*). Have I ever even thrown a speck of dirt at you since I brought you from Kezhakke Kalleda?

KARAMBI (*happily*). That's why I stood still and didn't run to the hut when you raised your stick. (*Lovingly touching and caressing Ceennan's face and head*) Lie down until your hangover is gone. After cooking supper, I'll boil some water and give you a hot steam bath. (*Sorrowfully*) You were beaten mercilessly by the landlord. (*She softly touches his shoulders and back, and wipes away her tears.*)

CEENNAN. Oh, please boil some water with tamarind and bathe my shoulders. I have to go to work tomorrow. (*Noticing that someone is coming from the right.*) Who's coming? (*To Karambi*) Is it Paramu Naayar of Nade Vadakkell's wife?

KARAMBI (*looking in that direction*). Yes.

Paramu Naayar's young wife enters from the right. She is dishevelled, wearing a dhoti, blouse, and towel. She is very sad.

KARAMBI. Why have you come now, at nightfall?

PARAMU NAAYAR'S WIFE (*sadly*). My son's father[43] hasn't come home yet.

CEENNAN. Where did he go? He was not with me when I went to eat at the bungalow. The bullocks were bathed and taken out by Teevan.

KARAMBI. The landlord beat him horribly. It was so painful! (*Paramu Naayar's wife cries.*)

CEENNAN. It's even more painful that he was beaten and then yoked instead of the bullock! I'm a slave so I'm supposed to take the Tamburaan's beatings.

PARAMU NAAYAR'S WIFE (*sobbing*). Ceennan Pulayan, we're all slaves. When looking for Paramu Chettan, I went to the market. Everyone there looked at me painfully, but no one said a single sympathetic

---

43 A wife never speaks aloud her husband's name since it is considered bad luck. Therefore, wives use a variety of indirect phrases to name their husbands, such as 'son's father,' or 'older brother.'

word to me. No one said that the landlord did anything wrong.

KARAMBI. If anyone did say anything, the landlord wouldn't allow him to live!

PARAMU NAAYAR'S WIFE. Isn't everyone who lives here in fear a slave? (*Controlling her sobbing*) It's distressing to not even see my husband. My son is crying out for him at home.

KARAMBI. I'm afraid he might have crossed the border to escape the humiliation of his yoking.

PARAMU NAAYAR'S WIFE (*crying*). I'm afraid he might consider suicide.

CEENNAN. Once a man was so afraid of a Tamburaan that he hanged himself. (*Paramu Naayar's wife is shocked.*) It's said that he was killed by the Tamburaan and *then* hanged. (*Paramu Naayar's wife lets out a cry.*)

KARAMBI. Please, god, don't let anything like that happen!

CEENNAN (*To Paramu Naayar's wife*). Be calm. Nothing like that will happen.

PARAMU NAAYAR'S WIFE. How can I be calm? Who else is there for me and my child to go to?

KARAMBI. It's true. Their families didn't approve of their marriage.

PARAMU NAAYAR'S WIFE. We've loved each other since we were children. We married in spite of his family's objections. In order to survive, I used to work for daily wages while he went to plough. (*With anger and sorrow.*) Now he can't work anymore! (*Cursing*) That bastard will suffer for this!

When they hear her words, Ceennan and Karambi become afraid, and look around to see whether anyone else has heard her. Teevan enters from the left.

PARAMU NAAYAR'S WIFE (*quickly crossing to Teevan*). Teeva, have you seen Paramu Cheetan?

TEEVAN. When I went to bathe the bullocks in the brook I saw him washing his body, and then going to Payilkalil. After that I saw him heading west, wearing Goopaalapilla's shirt and dhoti.

KARAMBI. I'll bet he's crossed the border.

CEENNAN. I heard they're doing military recruitment![44]

PARAMU NAAYAR'S WIFE. Joining would be better than bearing the

---

44 A reference to recruitment into the army for service in World War II.

landlord's brutality. (*Sorrowfully to Teevan*) It was you who yoked my husband and your father together.

TEEVAN (*feeling guilty*). While doing it, I was crying in my heart. If I had disobeyed the landlord, I too would have been beaten and kicked! Who was there to stop it?

CEENNAN. It's the duty of tenants to obey the Tamburaan.

PARAMU NAAYAR'S WIFE. I'll go and search for him in other huts. (*Exits left.*)

Ceennan goes inside the hut with his bundle of rice.

TEEVAN (*sitting on the bench and looking into the hut. He calls*) Niili? (*No answer. Karambi begins to feel anxious.*)

TEEVAN. Niili? (*Still no answer. Karambi remains silent.*)

TEEVAN (*calling loudly*). Niili? (*When there is no answer, he looks at Karambi*) Isn't she here?

KARAMBI (*distressed*). She didn't come home after work.

TEEVAN. Then where did she go?

KARAMBI. To collect her wages.

TEEVAN. Didn't mother go with her?

KARAMBI (*even more distressed*). Yes, but when they gave me my wages, the wrestler-Tamburaan told me to leave.

TEEVAN (*with anger*). Why did mother come home and leave her there?

KARAMBI. That Tamburaan told me she'd come with you when you came.

TEEVAN (*with frustration and anger*). Mother, you know how these Tamburaans behave!!!

KARAMBI. What could I do? What could I say to the wrestler-Tamburaan? (*She goes inside.*)

Teevan, totally frustrated with anger and sorrow, paces around in an agitated mood. He feels first sorrow, then anger. Different sounds come from various huts. Drumming is heard from the Poorkali Bhagavathi Temple. He continues to pace in a confused state. When a bewildered Niili enters from the left, Teevan bursts out with uncontrollable anger.

TEEVAN (*with a roaring voice*). Where were you all this time!!! (*Niili tries to say something*) . . . Did you go to the granary? (*She tries to speak, but he cuts her off with his uncontrollable anger.*) I'll kill you!!! I won't let you live . . . (*He races into the hut.*)

Niili is scared. The drumming gets louder. Teevan comes out of the hut with a sickle. Karambi rushes out after him and tries to grab the sickle. They struggle.

TEEVAN (*as if possessed by the fierce goddess, Kali*). Let go of me! I'll kill her!

KARAMBI (*frightened and crying*). Son, don't do anything wrong!

NIILI (*crying and scared*). They grabbed me and pulled . . .

TEEVAN. I'll cut your head off!! (*He pulls away from Karambi. She catches him again. They pull against each other. Ceennan comes out of the hut and stands near the door anxiously.*)

TEEVAN (*in the same state*). I'll cut off your head and go to the police station. (*He moves forward.*)

Paramu Naayar enters from the left. He blocks Teevan's way and forcefully grabs the sickle from him. Karambi and Ceennan are relieved.

PARAMU NAAYAR. Won't you be hanged if you chop her head off?

TEEVAN. I may be hanged. I'll take her head and surrender to the police.

PARAMU NAAYAR. Then why don't you chop off the head of the Tamburaan—he's the one who takes her and other women to the granary! You won't be hanged twice if you kill the landlord!

TEEVAN. She cheated on me!

PARAMU NAAYAR (*casting a meaningful look at Niili*). Is that right, Niili?

NIILI (*crying*). I didn't go there. When I was coming to the hut with my wages, the wrestler-Tamburaan and two other henchmen chased me and caught me near the big stream, and then took me to the granary. While this was happening the landlord was still standing in the front yard. But I escaped from the granary through the back door.

Paramu Naayar looks at Teevan. His anger melts. Ceennan and Karambi are relieved. A moment of silence. Niili sobs. With a smile, Paramu Naayar hands the sickle to Teevan. His expression says, 'If you want to kill, kill now.' Feeling guilty, Teevan turns away from the sickle.

PARAMU NAAYAR (*giving the sickle to Niili*). Put this inside. It's not for cutting heads. It's for cutting rice stalks.

Teevan is now totally calm. He feels guilty. Niili goes into the hut with the sickle. A moment of silence. The drumming reaches its climax and ends.

CEENNAN. It's drumming from the Poorkali Poti Temple.

PARAMU NAAYAR. It's a *keelikottu*.[45] It's a long time before the performance will begin. (*To Teevan*) Teeva, there was a custom among old Pulayans to cut off the head of a wife when she was raped by a Tamburaan.

CEENNAN. It's true. When I was a child, one time I saw a Pulayan of Kaithakootam cut off his wife's head and walk to the police with the bleeding head in his hands. Blood was dripping from the head. I got so scared!

PARAMU NAAYAR. Aren't those times gone? (*To Teevan*) Do you want to hold on to the past?

TEEVAN (*feeling guilty*). I couldn't control myself when I heard that she had gone to the landlord.

PARAMU NAAYAR. Don't be controlled! But cutting off your wife's head isn't the solution!

KARAMBI. There would have been a murder here unless you'd come.

Paramu Naayar sits on the bench. Ceennan crosses to him:

CEENNAN. Where did you go when you left the paddy field? Your wife was searching for you here. She says your son is crying for you. (*Paramu Naayar sits thoughtfully silent.*)

KARAMBI. We thought you'd crossed the border.

PARAMU NAAYAR. Where would I go if I left this place?

CEENNAN. Weren't you humiliated?

PARAMU NAAYAR. It's the landlord who should feel humiliated for yoking and ploughing with us instead of his bullocks!

TEEVAN. I saw you heading west.

PARAMU NAAYAR. I went to Vallikkunnam. (*Ceennan and Karambi are frightened.*)[46]

TEEVAN. There's a rumour that the police are torturing everyone there.

PARAMU NAAYAR. It's true. The police torture everyone who's suspected of being a labour union worker or their relative. They're even attacking their homes. When the police entered Chalithara Kunjachan's hut, the first thing they did was to take their *lathis* and break the clay pot filled with water. They took all the dried tapioca

---

45 Part of the preliminary drumming before a *kathakali* dance-drama performance during the local temple festival.

46 Vallikkunnam is Tooppil Bhaasi's birthplace, i.e., he went to see Bhaasi. They're frightened because they know he's a communist wanted by the police and in hiding.

they were keeping in their storeroom and mixed it with animal shit. Kunjachan's father, old Chalithara Kunjali Pulayan, was kicked and beaten as if he was a drum. No one knows what's happened to Chelakkottu Kunnuraaman, his wife, and their five children. Bhaasi—the one who's in hiding—his father and younger brother were both beaten in the yard of their home! The police showered Bhaasi's mother with foul language, and then chased her around their house.

CEENNAN (*fearfully*). My god!! (*Karambi is frozen still with fear.*)

PARAMU NAAYAR. There's much more to tell. There, no one would dare to plough the land with workers! There all the women of workers' families sleep safely in their huts.

KARAMBI. Hearing what you say, my hands and legs are trembling.

PARAMU NAAYAR. The trembling of the Pulayans is over in that area!

TEEVAN. Why did you go to Vallikkunnam?

PARAMU NAAYAR. To see someone who's in hiding.

CEENNAN (*afraid*). Ayyoo!

TEEVAN. Did you see him?

PARAMU NAAYAR. Yes, I did.

KARAMBI. My god! If the police saw you . . .

CEENNAN. Why did you go where there's so much trouble?

PARAMU NAAYAR. To be able to walk straight and tall, like a man with a backbone. To not bend anymore under the yoke!

TEEVAN. What did they say?

PARAMU NAAYAR (*in a low voice*). I have brought someone who will tell all.

KARAMBI/CEENNAN (*together, anxiously*). Yeh!

PARAMU NAAYAR (*softly*). The one who's in hiding. (*Ceennan and Karambi are frightened.*)

TEEVAN (*looking around, softly*). Who?

PARAMU NAAYAR (*softly*). Bhaasi. (*Ceennan and Karambi are even more frightened.*)

CEENNAN. Ayyoo! Isn't this going to create problems?

PARAMU NAAYAR (*smiling*). Why are you so afraid? The landlord is the one who should be afraid.

CEENNAN. If anyone knows about this, the police will come here! My god!

PARAMU NAAYAR. Well, don't tell anyone yet.

KARAMBI (*anxiously in a low voice*). It's rumoured that he fooled the Police.

PARAMU NAAYAR. That's true. People like us hide them. We'll hide the person I brought with me for a few days.

CEENNAN (*surprised*). We?

PARAMU NAAYAR. Yes. Tonight and tomorrow we'll use Ceennan Pulayan's hut.

CEENNAN. Ayyoo!

KARAMBI. The four of us are supposed to cook, eat, and sleep in this hut. (*Teevan thinks.*)

CEENNAN. Ayyoo! Not here! I'm afraid!

KARAMBI. He's supposed to eat, drink, and live here?

PARAMU NAAYAR. Give him a share of what you have. If you're starving, give him a share of that!

CEENNAN. I can't make up my mind.

TEEVAN (*thinking*). My mind is made up! (*To Paramu Naayar*) Where is he?

PARAMU NAAYAR. Over there, in the tapioca plants.

TEEVAN. Then go and get him. (*Ceennan and Karambi look anxiously at each other.*)

PARAMU NAAYAR. I'll go get him now. Teeva, I sent someone to call Kalakkattu Parameeswaran Naayar and Thandasserry. We'll sit together. (*Looking into the hut*) Niili? (*Niili answers, coming to the door.*) Did you hear what we said? We'll have one more for dinner. What do we have?

NIILI. Tapioca and rice.

PARAMU NAAYAR. More than enough! I'll go and get him now. (*He exits.*)

Ceennan and Karambi are distressed. Ceennan walks around anxiously. Teevan looks to the right to see if anyone is coming. All look to the left.

KARAMBI (*after a pause, thinking*). Where will he sleep?

NIILI. After dinner is cooked, we can put the hearth stones outside, give him our mats, and we can sleep outside. The moon is yet to rise.

TEEVAN. Mother, do what Niili says. But Father can sleep inside too.

CEENNAN. Teeva, be careful. If anything happens to us, he should be safely protected.

Everyone looks to the left—alert. They hear the breaking of the branches of a tapioca plant. They stand frozen in tableau. After awhile, and while they are frozen, Paramu Naayar enters as if nothing has happened. He laughs. When they see him they react suddenly.

PARAMU NAAYAR. Why are you holding your breath? (*Crosses to Ceennan with a smile.*) Ceennan Pulayan, why don't you dance and sing? (*Suspiciously*) Did you drink toddy today?

CEENNAN. My hangover is gone!

Paramu Naayar smiles. Ceennan and the others look at each other, and then look around to try and see the man who's in hiding.

PARAMU NAAYAR. Teeva, give me a beedi.[47]

Teevan gives him a beedi. Paramu Naayar takes the kerosene lamp and lights it. Suddenly he blows out the lamp. Total darkness. The light of the burning beedi is all that can be seen. Its red glow moves to the left and disappears. Immediately it reappears on stage, along with the light of a second beedi, and the two slowly cross toward the right, disappearing into the hut. Teevan lights a match and the lamp. Ceennan, Karambi, and Niili are looking into the hut. Teevan too looks into the hut. After a few moments Paramu Naayar comes out of the hut, smoking a beedi.

PARAMU NAAYAR (*smiling*). Ceennan Pulayan, go inside and say hello. Speak softly. (*Ceennan cautiously goes near the doorway and looks inside, as if seeing a terrorist.*)

TEEVAN (*to Karambi and Niili*). What are you two looking at? Go on and prepare dinner.

PARAMU NAAYAR. Karamban Pulaki, take this lamp inside. The moon is rising. There's enough light here to see.

Karambi goes inside with the lamp, followed by Ceennan. Niili walks to the rear of the hut, as if to enter by the back door. The onstage light fades as the lamp is taken inside. The light comes from the hut, and the rising moon. The shadows of Paramu Naayar and Teevan.

PARAMU NAAYAR. We'll go inside when Parameeswaran Naayar, Payikkatu Goopaalapilla, and the others come. To avoid suspicion, Ceennan, Niili, and Teevan should talk and sing while you're sitting in front of the hut.

TEEVAN. There's no problem tonight, but tomorrow during the day the neighbours will come.

---

47 An inexpensive hand-rolled smoke.

PARAMU NAAYAR. Close the door tomorrow. Only for the day. If anyone asks, tell them that you've resurfaced the floor with dung water and it needs to dry. Eventually, we can inform others about what's happening. Then perhaps he can hide in a different hut each day.

Parameeswaran Naayar, Thandasserry, and Goopaalapilla arrive. In the moonlight their shadows are visible one by one. Paramu Naayar whispers to each of them, and then sends them into the hut.

PARAMU NAAYAR. Call Ceennan Pulayan to come here.

Teevan looks in both directions, like a guard, and then into the hut.

TEEVAN. Father, bring that *udukku* drum. (*A few seconds later, Ceennan comes out with the drum.*)

CEENNAN. Why do you want this now?

TEEVAN. To play and sing. For *them* to hear. Father, go sneak around the nearby huts and see whether there's anything suspicious.

CEENNAN. That's a good idea. (*Exits right.*)

Teevan sits down on the bench and plays the drum. Paramu Naayar's wife enters from the left. She is extremely upset since she has not found her husband.

PARAMU NAAYAR'S WIFE (*sobbing*). I searched everywhere. No one has seen him since this afternoon.

TEEVAN (*smiling slightly*). Don't worry. He hasn't gone away.

PARAMU NAAYAR'S WIFE. Teevan is only saying this to console me.

TEEVAN. No.

PARAMU NAAYAR'S WIFE. (*anxiously*). Do you know where he is? (*Teevan remains silent*). Where is he? (*Teevan still remains silent*). If you know, please tell me. Let me have some peace of mind.

TEEVAN (*reflecting for a moment*). Sit on this bench for awhile. (*He goes into the hut*).

Paramu Naayar's wife reflects for a few seconds, and then sits down on the bench. Her sorrowful face is visible in the moonlight. Teevan comes out of the hut with a lamp, puts it on the bench, and then exits left. Paramu Naayar's wife becomes even more anxious. Paramu Naayar enters from the hut. She looks at him with surprise and stands up.

PARAMU NAAYAR'S WIFE. Were you here when I came earlier?

PARAMU NAAYAR. No. I only just reached here.

PARAMU NAAYAR'S WIFE. (*suspiciously*). Why were you sitting inside?

(*Paramu Naayar doesn't answer. In the same tone*) Have you been hiding from the Tamburaan?

PARAMU NAAYAR. I would never hide out of fear of the landlord. But I might hide from the police.

WIFE. What do you mean? I don't understand any of this.

PARAMU NAAYAR. I'll explain everything to you soon. But for now, please go.

WIFE. Let's go together. Our son is crying out for you.

Paramu Naayar stands still and silent—full of emotion.

WIFE. Let's go home.

PARAMU NAAYAR. You go on alone. Tell our son not to cry. If I do not return, you too must not cry. If you begin crying, it will go on forever.

WIFE. I was born to cry. I cried before I was married. And today I cried when the Tamburaan of the bungalow beat you and ploughed with you instead of his bullocks. (*She cries.*)

PARAMU NAAYAR. I'm engaged in work that in the future will prevent you and our son from crying. I'll explain it later. Go to our son now and console him.

WIFE (*standing still as if she suspects something*). Exactly what are you saying?

PARAMU NAAYAR. I'm organizing workers and farmers to fight against oppression.

WIFE. You know what happened in Vallikkunnam and elsewhere?

PARAMU NAAYAR. Yes. We're going to join them.

WIFE. There the Reserve Police harrassed and even mutilated the women.

PARAMU NAAYAR. You too might face the same!

WIFE. But who will look after both my son and I? (*Paramu Naayar remains silent.*) Can we let him starve? Shouldn't he be sent to school? (*Paramu Naayar is still silent*). Even if I'm willing to work, who'll give me a job?

PARAMU NAAYAR (*emotionally*). Don't feel that I do not love you. (*Gently*) If it's impossible for you to survive, then go ahead and marry someone else.

She is stunned. She looks at him and bursts out crying.

PARAMU NAAYAR. There's no point in living as if we're dead for the sake of an ideology. I've dedicated my life to the cause and I won't turn back from that.

He walks aheads and looks in the opposite direction, as if trying to avoid his crying wife. She controls her crying, goes to her husband, and touches his shoulder.

PARAMU NAAYAR (*turning to face her*). My younger brother isn't married. I'll ask him to feed both you and my son. (*His wife cries.*) Go home now. (*She continues to cry.*) Won't you obey what I've said? (*She looks pitifully at Paramu Naayar, and exits to the right, crying. Paramu Naayar stands frustrated. He takes a long breath.*) Teevan! (*Teevan enters from the left.*) Where did your father go?

TEEVAN. He went off somewhere in the neighbourhood.

PARAMU NAAYAR. Call Niili. Then sit here and talk loudly. (*He enters the hut.*)

TEEVAN (*sitting on the bench, he begins to drum, and then calls Niili. Niili answers.*) Come here for awhile. (*Niili enters. Smiling*) You're afraid, aren't you?

NIILI (*quietly*). I thought my head would be offered to the police Tamburaans!

TEEVAN (*laughing*). I thought my head would be hanging from a rope!

NIILI (*gestures that those inside will hear them*). Speak quietly.

TEEVAN. We're supposed to speak loudly. It's to cover the conversation they're having inside. Sit here. (*He catches her hand and pulls her onto the bench.*) Let's sing a song. (*He begins to drum.*)

NIILI (*as if accusing him*). You're still out to cut off my head!

TEEVAN. It's all because of my overflowing love for you. When I thought you'd been seduced, I thought of killing us both. Dear Niili, if the landlord and his 'wrestler' say *anything* off-colour to you, curse them at once.

NIILI (*mocking*). Now you're becoming very courageous!

TEEVAN. Did you see that man who went into our hut at dark? At that moment I became courageous. (*Laughs. Niili too laughs. Ceennan enters from the right. Niili stands up.*)

CEENNAN (*quietly*). Don't laugh too loudly, my children.

TEEVAN. We can laugh aloud, father. Sit down here.

CEENNAN. Aay, Teeva, the man who came to our hut wasn't who we thought he was. He's only twenty-four years old. He looks innocent. He caught hold of my hand and made me sit next to him. That's the first time in my life a Tamburaan has touched[48] me without beating me.

48 The word for 'touch' (*toottutiintuka*) also means 'to pollute' by touching.

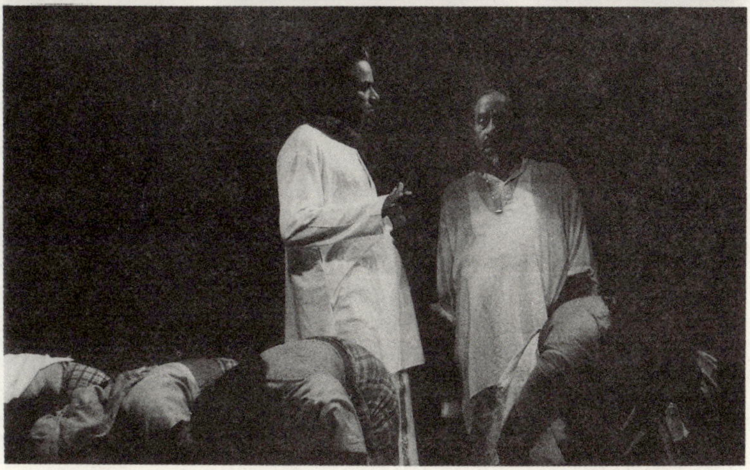

Above The Actress and Stage Manager lead the company in singing a song which sets the mood of the opening scene. *Below* The Landlord and Nannu Naayar enjoy watching and discussing the backsides of the women planters.

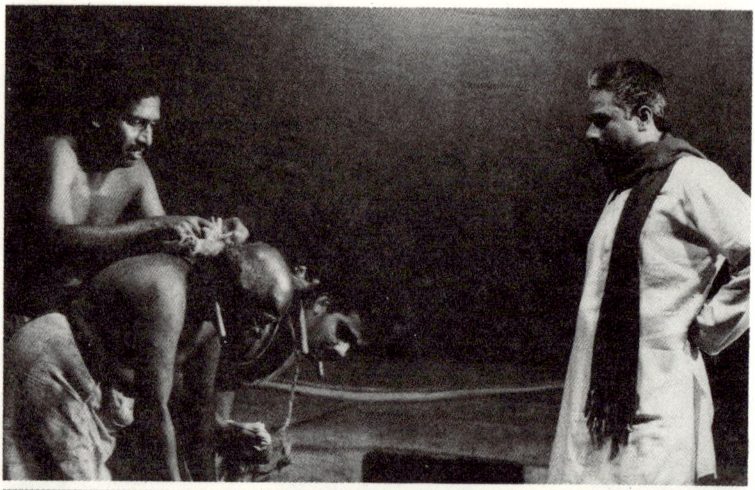

Above The Landlord forces Teevan to yoke together his father, Ceennan, and Paramu Naayar, and to plough the paddy field. *Below* Niili and her husband, Teevan, sing a romantic love song while Bhaasi holds the meeting inside Ceennan's hut.

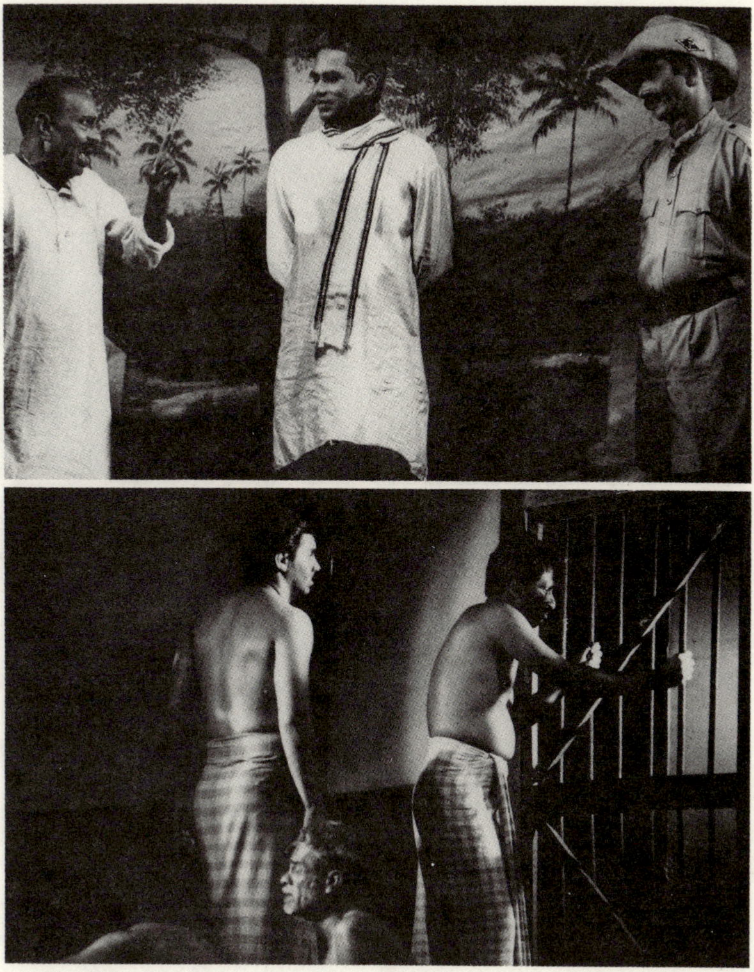

Above Nannu Naayar trying to impress the Reserve Policeman who has just arrived to question him. *Below* Inside the jail cell. Paramu Naayar and Teevan watch in horror as Goopaalapilla is tortured in front of them.

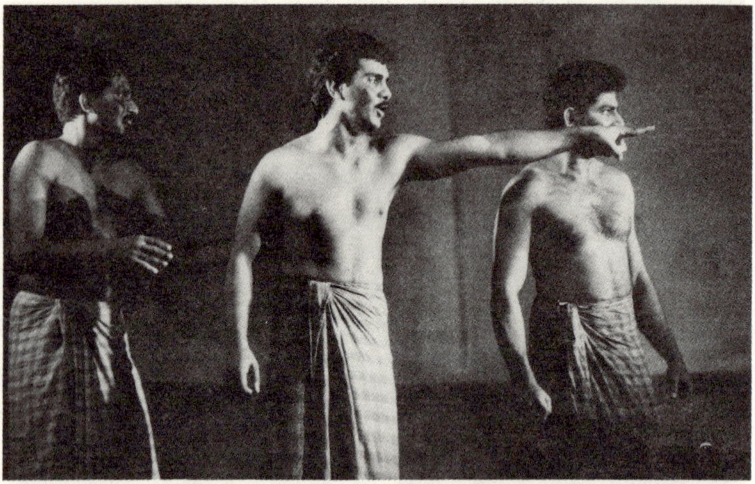

Above Paramu Naayar: 'Our voices will be heard even after we die. They are the voices of revolution.' *Below* The Stage Manager and Actress end the play by leading the entire company, with raised fists, in singing their song of revolution.

(*Teevan and Niili laugh.*) He asked me all about our family.

TEEVAN. Father, sit here. Let's sing for him.

Teevan sits on the bench and starts drumming a special song. The three of them sing a folk song. When the song is about to end, Nannu Naayar enters with another goonda or ruffian. Ceennan and the others are frightened.

NANNU NAAYAR. What! You're singing without a lamp or light?

TEEVAN. I'll get a lamp (*enters the hut*).

NANNU NAAYAR. Hey, Ceennan! Is it good to disobey the Tamburaan? (*Ceennan feels uneasy. Teevan enters with a lamp. The stage is fully lit.*)

NANNU NAAYAR. So tell me, is it right to disobey the Tamburaan?

TEEVAN. I've never done anything against the Tamburaan.

NANNU NAAYAR. You haven't, have you? Shall I produce proof, right here, right now?

Ceennan, Teevan, and Niili are silent. They look at each other, as if afraid that the newcomers might know that there's someone hiding in the hut.

NANNU NAAYAR. Why are you all keeping quiet? (*Ceennan, Teevan, and Niili remain silent.*) I'll prove it right now. (*He walks nears the door of the hut where Niili is standing. Teevan and Ceenan are afraid.*) (*Pointing at Niili.*) I told her to clean out the granary. This proud woman walked out and didn't do her work. (*Coughs. Ceennan and Teevan are relieved.*) In order to avoid provoking Tamburaan, we had called her and sent her there to work. But this proud woman ran out the back door. Now, isn't that disobeying Tamburaan?

NIILI. I left because it was getting dark.

NANNU NAAYAR. Ceennan, did you hear her deny it? (*Laughs*) Say, in the past, when a slave girl menstruated for the first time, didn't the Tamburaan always allow her to stay in a hut outside the compound? After her fourth bath, didn't she go to the Tamburaan first? (*He coughs. Ceennan remains silent.*)

TEEVAN. But isn't that custom being changed, wrestler-Tamburaan?

NANNU NAAYAR. Oh, do you mean communism has arrived here? Haven't you heard stories about places where communism has taken root? Those who were spreading communism in Vallikunnu, Aathinad, and Vallikavil were stamped out by police actions. Some of them are still in jail receiving beatings three times a day. They'll soon die from coughing (*coughs*).

GOONDA (*to Ceenan and the others*). The wrestler coughs because of his bouts with Electric Mytheen.

NANNU NAAYAR. It's rumoured that those who escaped from the police have gone to Madras and Bombay. (*Laughs loudly while coughing. Ceennan and Nannu Naayar also laugh. Teevan and Niili look at each other, and control their laughter. Their laughs have an alternative meaning.*) None of these 'isms' can be allowed in our Suranad, Pulayans. Did anyone who's been in hiding come here? None of them should be allowed to stop here. (*He takes a plate and bends it as if indicating what would happen if someone was allowed to come. Seriously*) Your Tamburaan is angrily waiting over there. He said that he's going to evict you and burn your hut! But I said not to do such things, and said Niili had only run away because of her impudence. I promised him I'd take her back to clean the granary today. (*Looking at Niili as if she didn't matter*) Come! (*He walks to the left, expecting her to follow him.*)

TEEVAN. Tonight itself? (*Nannu Naayar turns back.*) Tomorrow morning she and I will both come to clean.

Nannu Naayar laughs. The Goonda joins him.

NANNU NAAYAR. You too! (*Looking at the Goonda*) Did you hear the nonsense he's speaking? He's a fool who doesn't know what the word 'cleaning' means!

TEEVAN. She won't come tonight.

NANNU NAAYAR (*surprised*). Ceennan, did you hear your son's impudent words?

CEENNAN. What can I do about that, Tamburaan? She's his wife. If you want, you can take my old wife with you.

NANNU NAAYAR (*angrily*). He's not that desperate yet! (*Casting an angry look at them, he exits, followed by the Goonda.*)

TEEVAN (*after a pause, to Niili*). If supper is ready, please serve it now. Take the lamp inside.

Niili goes into the hut with the lamp. Teevan and Ceennan are in the shadows. Teevan looks in the direction in which Nannu Naayar exited.

CEENNAN (*to his son*). Will we be evicted?

TEEVAN. Maybe those inside heard what was said. Let's do what they suggest.

Paramu Naayar enters from the hut.

PARAMU NAAYAR. We'll decide what to do later if they actually come to evict you, Ceennan Pulayan. (*To Teevan*) Thandasserry and the others and I are going out. We've some things to do.

TEEVAN. Tonight?

PARAMU NAAYAR. Yes. We've decided to hold a march and meeting to protest against the use of torture. We need to prepare posters and post them. We'll be publicizing it with megaphones, and we'll visit a few homes. (*Looking into the hut*) Let's go, Parameeswaran Naayar.

CEENNAN. Are the Tamburaans permitting you to hold the meeting?

PARAMU NAAYAR. Who needs their permission? Marches and meetings aren't banned by the government. (*To Teevan*) Teevan, don't come with us. You should stay here on watch.

TEEVAN. I'll sleep outside, and father can sleep inside. (*Paramu Naayar looks at Teevan meaningfully.*)

TEEVAN (*understanding*). I'll keep a knife under my pillow.

Paramu Naayar smiles. Goopaalapilla and Parameeswaran Naayar come out of the hut, and leave with Paramu Naayar.

CEENNAN (*thinking for a few moments, he goes to Teevan and says quietly*). Where did you put the sickle?

Teevan looks at his father and smiles. The lights fade. The stage is lit by moonlight. Teevan is sleeping on the bench. Karambi and Niili lie on the ground on mats. It is so silent you could hear a pin drop. The noise of night birds. Late night.

An announcement is heard through a megaphone:

Inkulaab-Zindabad.[49]

Dear people. In our locality also there is an awakening against landlordism! Be prepared to save the purity of our mothers and sisters and to escape from the tyranny of the landlords. Come join the protest march that begins from Poika Plains. Attend the meeting at the market set for tomorrow night. Come protest against the police and landlord violence!

When the announcement is heard, Teevan, then Niili, and then Karambi each get up, and listen carefully. Ceennan enters from the hut with his sickle. Another announcement is heard:

Dear people! In Vallikkunnathu where the Reserve Police were stationed, they tortured everyone. They arrested and tortured the relatives of our comrades in hiding! Come to the meeting to protest

---

49 'Long live the revolution'.

against these actions!

Another announcement from another direction:

The police and landlords are incensed. They're harrassing our communist party workers who've not been banned. The police have gone on a mad rampage in Aathinad, Vallikkavu, Karthikappilli, Ennakkatte, and Vallikkunnath! Be prepared to participate in the march and the meeting. Down with landlordism! Down with police violence!

Another announcement is heard:

Listen to some good news! Comrade M. N. Govindhan has escaped from jail!!

The announcements echo in the hills, and come to an end. A cock crows from a distance.

ACT THREE

Scene 1

To the left, the eastern side of a vast paddy field. A canal from a pond. Three-fourths of the canal is visible on stage. The yellow light just after sunrise is spreading across the stage.

OFFSTAGE VOICE (*a man howls and shouts*). They're catching fish at Kizhakada canal! Hurry! Hurry up! We have the right to fish! We will not allow the landlords to control government lands intended for public use! No secret auctions or private registrations! Come out to fish!

Again howling voices and calls. Someone returns a call. From the right a Kuthiyotta song is heard.[50]

As the song progresses, a group of men enter singing from the right. Among them are Paramu Naayar, Parameeswaran Naayar, Goopaalapilla, Thandasserry, Ceennan, Teevan, and others. A group of women follows them, including Karambi, Niili, the wives of both Paramu Naayar and Goopaalapilla, and others. The women hold nets and ottaal with which to catch fish. The men have long nets over their shoulders. The men dance rhythmically in a variety of steps and sing, eventually moving toward the pond offstage. In between the verses the women stand behind the dancing men and shout out calls.

(*Refrain*). Taananna taanaana tannaana–taanai
taananna naanaana tannaana

Bhadrakali, the warrior goddess—
the village deity set forth to view the land.

(*Refrain*)

Without a pearl decorated umbrella, without a lamp,
Having bathed in the forest river and wearing a wild flower.

(*Refrain*)

Distributing property wearing a musk *tilaka*,
generous and compassionate, dancing in ecstasy.

(*Refrain*)
Jasmines, black pepper plants, coconut palms

50 *Kuthiyottam* is a ritual performance which takes places in Bhadrakali temples.

with tender leaves, and an umbrella sized yam.

(Refrain)

Golden bunches of rice grain
stood filling the fresh paddy fields.

(Refrain)

In your sacred presence, circumambulating,
people dance in all possible ways, spreading
grace all over.

(Refrain)

With song, peacocks dance, joining heads together,
being playful, crossing flags, they approach you.

(Refrain)

After the group exits, Tamburaan, Nannu Naayar, and a servant enter from the opposite side and look in the direction of the pond. Along with the howls and shouts, the sounds of men fishing in the canal can be heard as they call out

Push back the bushes!
Cast the net over there.
Catch that one!
Bring the *ottaal*!

There is general laughter and an expression of exuberance. Meanwhile, the Tamburaan and Nannu Naayar speak.

NANNU NAAYAR. Do you know what song they sang before they started fishing?

JANMI. *Kuthiyotta*'s song.

NANNU NAAYAR. At one time there were ritual sacrifices in the Bhadrakali temple. There were even human sacrifices. When these rituals were stopped, *kuthiyottam* was introduced to replace the sacrifices. When someone performs *kuthiyottam* he pierces both sides of his chest with pieces of cane. Blood comes out on both sides! It's a ritual with real blood.

JANMI. It's time *kuthiyottam* was stopped. Instead, these people should be sacrificed alive! What's their justification for catching fish from a pond whose fishing rights have been auctioned off? Do what I tell you. Draft a petition for the Adoor police. I'll write a cover letter to the Inspector. They won't eat a single fish they've caught today!

NANNU NAAYAR. Say that they've been inspired and sent by the communists! And say that Tambi, Puthupalli, Bhaasi, and Perur who went underground are openly staying here, even today! And that M. N. who escaped from jail is also here!

JANMI. I'll include it all! Go, get ready, and meet me at my house. (*The servant exits. Nannu Naayar looks left and gestures with his eyes. The Tamburaan looks left. Suddenly he turns upstage, his back to the audience. Nannu Naayar also turns upstage. Niili enters from the left. When she sees the Tamburaan, she ducks her head and exits right quickly. Nannu Naayar turns his head, and sees that she's gone.*)

NANNU NAAYAR. All clear! She's gone. (*Tamburaan turns downstage.*) Oh, excellent!

JANMI. What's excellent?

NANNU NAAYAR. Turning backward and freezing! If she's unwilling, then I'll get a willing woman. That's excellent, isn't it? (*The landlord grunts his approval*). It's shameful! (*The landlord looks at Nannu Naayar.*) No, no, not you, her! She's shameful! She passed by us without even bowing her head. (*Noticing that someone else is coming from the left*) Tamburaan, look who's coming! Did you see that he's walking straight toward us without taking a detour? He's the arrogant one who's trying to establish communism here!

Paramu Naayar enters, neither arrogantly nor humbly.

JANMI. Paramu? (*Paramu Naayar turns back just as he was about to exit on the right.*) Are you the one who's prompting the people to catch fish from this pond?

PARAMU NAAYAR. It's not me. You know that every year it's the usual routine to come and catch fish from this pond. After all, it's a public pond.

JANMI. Didn't you know that I purchased the fishing rights to this pond for one year at public auction?

PARAMU NAAYAR. No, we didn't know.

NANNU NAAYAR (*with mocking laughter*). Is it necessary to inform you at your hut that there's going to be an auction of fishing rights for a public pond?

PARAMU NAAYAR. No, it's not necessary. It would be enough if a notice was posted at the administrative office.

JANMI. I'm unwilling to do that!

NANNU NAAYAR. He's unwilling to do that!

PARAMU NAAYAR (*to the landlord*). Does the government need your permission to post a notice?

NANNU NAAYAR. It's his government! (*Paramu Naayar laughs.*) Oh, did you see his mocking laughter!

PARAMU NAAYAR (*to the landlord*). Tell your government that it can't auction off the rights to public ponds that are used by the people for bathing and washing their animals! Poor people have a right to eat the minnows they catch from that pond, with their tapioca!

JANMI. You won't eat your tapioca with the minnows you've caught in that pond!

PARAMU NAAYAR. We will. But we won't allow the wealthy or the landholders to illegally register or auction public property. Public lands should be given with full legal registration to the homeless so that they can at least build a hut!

JANMI (*with a mocking laugh*). So you think you'll get such legal registrations!

NANNU NAAYAR (*laughing loudly*). Legally registered? Legally registered!!

PARAMU NAAYAR. Don't doubt it. What we want is to put a maximum ceiling on the amount of land any landlord can hold, and distribute the excess land to the homeless.[51]

Both the landlord and Nannu Naayar laugh loudly.

JANMI. The lands I own were not earned by your fathers!

PARAMU NAAYAR. They were earned by the sweat of our fathers, and we'll get them back!

JANMI. Don't you know what's happened at Vallikunnath?

PARAMU NAAYAR. I know very, very well.

NANNU NAAYAR (*surprised*). This Naayar boy is a radical! (*He looks at Paramu Naayar*) Don't forget that you're the keeper of his bullocks!

PARAMU NAAYAR. I *was* the keeper of his bullocks. Never again will I bend a shoulder to bear the yoke in place of his bullock!

The landlord glares angrily at Paramu Naayar. Then he looks at Nannu Naayar, indicating with his eyes that he should give him a beating. Nannu Naayar poses like a wrestler, and crosses to Paramu Naayar. Paramu Naayar stands completely still, ignoring him. When he sees that he won't move, Nannu Naayar turns back. He lifts his leg to kick

---

51 See Appendix regarding land reform

Paramu Naayar, but when he sees that Paramu Naayar doesn't move an inch, he cries out . . .

NANNU NAAYAR. Ayyyooo! I've got a muscle cramp! (*Paramu Naayar stands still, smiling. Massaging his muscles, and telling the landlord*) I got a muscle cramp.

PARAMU NAAYAR. Is it better?

NANNU NAAYAR (*changing his tactics*). My dear Paramu, Naayars like us are never disobedient.

PARAMU NAAYAR. We shouldn't be foot-lickers.

NANNU NAAYAR. Are you saying I follow him around like his dog? Does a dog get muscle cramps?

PARAMU NAAYAR. Your muscles aren't cramped.

NANNU NAAYAR. Hey! My muscles did too cramp! I was a wrestler. And now I'm his bodyguard. There's nothing to be ashamed of in that. He's an aristocratic Naayar.

PARAMU NAAYAR. Right! (*Exits.*)

NANNU NAAYAR. Oh, he's such a rebel! (*To the landlord*) I would have shown him if my muscles hadn't cramped!

The group of people fishing are laughing and howling again. The landlord and Nannu Naayar look in their direction. Niili enters from the right. She carries a cooking pot for the minnows. The landlord and Nannu Naayar turn upstage as before. She exits. Again the howls of the fishermen. The landlord and Nannu Naayar look off again.

NANNU NAAYAR (*to the landlord*). They're not howling at us. Let's go so you can write your letter to the Inspector Tamburaan.

The landlord exits to the right. Nannu Naayar follows. The fishermen continue howling and laughing.

Scene 2

A deserted area thick with shrubs. There is a big brook and a small river flowing nearby. A small dam to one side of the river. The sun is sinking in the west. The golden light gives splendour to the atmosphere.

On the right, facing the west, are eight to ten persons sitting on the ground, in a secret meeting. They are Goopaalapilla, Parameeswaran Naayar, Thandasserry Raaghavan, Teevan and others. Paramu Naayar and Chelakkottethu Kunnuraaman are standing behind them. They are looking to see whether anyone else is coming. Their faces glow in the golden light. One man, Bhaasi, is speaking to them. He can't be seen because of the shrubs.

BHAASI'S VOICE (*off*). Remember that this is a 'life and death' situation. Our primary goal is to end tenancy and landlordism. A movement like this has already begun in different parts of India including Thelunkana. Do you know what's happening in these places?

ONE MAN. We don't know the details.

VOICE (*off*). Kunnuraaman, one of those who was a leader in the Vallikkunnu strike, is standing right here. (*Everyone turns and looks at Kunnuraaman.*) Kunnuraaman's small house was demolished by the police and their goondas. Now he's in hiding with his wife and five children. The comrade himself should explain what happened there.

KUNNURAAMAN. It wasn't only our house that was destroyed, but also those of Chalithara Kunjuchan and Teevan. (*He points to the comrade who is hiding behind a shrub.*) The police attacked our houses a number of times, including his. They tortured everyone in sight. In other places too the same thing happened.

TEEVAN. Where else in this area did the police continue their attacks?

KUNNURAAMAN. At Karthikapalli, Mahadevikat Thottukadavil Vasu's house was attacked. There the police tortured Thambi-master's nephew, Balakrishnan Thambi. They tortured that eighteen year old boy until he was spitting blood and passed out!

PARAMEESWARAN NAAYAR. Damned police! What they did must be avenged.

The western sky reddens. Red light falls on their faces as if it reflects their anger.

KUNNURAAMAN. The police 'insulted' Sarojini, Vasu's sister. If I keep on telling you all that happened, it will never end. Aadinad G. Karthikeyan's father was tortured. Karthikeyan's younger brother was arrested and locked up. In jail he was beaten and eventually completely disfigured.

PARAMU NAAYAR. I've heard that the police have also attacked Vallikkavil N. Sreedharan's family. When his mother died he couldn't even see her body since the police were guarding it!

KUNNURAAMAN. I saw N.S. just before coming here. He told me all about the pathetic situation at Comrade Thambi's home in Pallana. There the police arrested and locked up Subhadrama and her newborn baby.

RAAGHAVAN. I heard that the baby was less than three months old!

KUNNURAAMAN. It's true. Thambi's brothers are all in hiding. Now only his parents, his older sister and her daughter, Ammini, remain at home. Congressmen and the well-to-do have segregated his family from everyone else. A neighbour doesn't dare even loan them a match to start a fire.

GOOPAALAPILLA. Isn't there anyone who is sympathetic in that area?

KUNNURAAMAN. Yes. On some mornings members of the family find packets of rice, pepper, or salt in their house compound. Our people are there, but they're afraid to openly help the family.

COMRADE'S VOICE. In brief, we're on a battleground fighting tenancy and landlordism. We have to fight against both the police and the military. Ours is a very risky path. Some of us may never see each other again. Our guides are the martyrs who have sacrificed their lives to machine guns and scaffolds from Kayoor to Punnapra-Vayalar. How many of you are willing to take this risk?

ALL. We all are!

The sky is dark red in color. It is reflected on all their faces.

COMRADE'S VOICE. Shall we part company now?

PARAMU NAAYAR. The landlord sent an agent with his petition against fishing.

COMRADE'S VOICE. You can be sure that the police will come.

GOOPAALAPILLA. What should we do?

COMRADE'S VOICE. Don't allow yourselves to be arrested.

TEEVAN. But what if they attack our homes?

COMRADE'S VOICE. If they insult the women in your families, use any means possible to resist them.

KUNNURAAMAN (*enthusiastically*). Don't simply say we should resist—anyone who attacks a woman shouldn't leave there alive!

RAAGHAVAN. He's right! If we don't retaliate, they'll rape our mothers and sisters!

PARAMEESWARAN NAAYAR. I agree with both Thandasserry and Comrade Kunnuraaman.

Ceennan rushes in, afraid, and out of breath.

PARAMU NAAYAR. What's wrong?

CEENNAN. The police have come!

PARAMU NAAYAR. Where?

CEENNAN. They're at Tamburaan's house. There are two cars full of police. Some of them have guns. They came early this evening. I was at Tamburaan's house when they got there.

TEEVAN. Did any of them see you leave to come here?

CEENNAN. I'm not a fool. Just like usual I left after work and walked home. Niili told me you were somewhere near the dam. (*To the comrade in hiding*) I only came to warn you.

KUNNURAAMAN (*thoughtfully*). Since they came so early, why haven't they started searching for offenders?

CEENNAN. Some of them went to the toddy shop.

PARAMEESWARAN NAAYAR. That's to jack up their courage!

GOOPAALAPILLA. The landlord owns the license for that toddy shop. The police will probably get the toddy free of charge!

COMRADE'S VOICE. Ceennan can go home.

CEENNAN (*crossing to the hiding place. With love and respect*). Be careful!

COMRADE'S VOICE (*happily*). I'll be careful, comrade.

CEENNAN. While I was working, I heard the landlord repeating your name several times.

COMRADE'S VOICE. Don't worry about it. I'll be careful. You should go.

PARAMU NAAYAR. Go quietly.

Ceennan bows to the Comrade and exits.

COMRADE'S VOICE (*suddenly affected by emotion*). Who is to be feared when there are people like Ceennan here who provide those of us hiding with safety and love?

RAAGHAVAN. Is it true that M. N. escaped from jail?

COMRADE'S VOICE. Don't doubt it. He's in contact with the party leadership. Our party workers have been inspired by M. N.'s escape and A. K. G.'s release when he pleaded his own court case.

KUNNURAAMAN. It drove our enemies mad!

The sun is sinking. Light fades.

PARAMU NAAYAR. It's getting dark. I'll take you to your next hiding place.

COMRADE'S VOICE. I can go to my shelter. I've got my courier.

TEEVAN. Who's that?

COMRADE'S VOICE. Don't you know who a 'courier' is, comrade? He's the one who maps out my secret route. With the help of our co-workers, he studies all possible routes and tracks the movements of the police. Then he recommends a safe route for each of us who is underground. Some comrades are called 'techmen.' Their duties are to deliver activity reports from the local organizations to the central bodies, and vice versa. These are some of the ways our secret revolutionary activities are carried out. Revolutionaries are not those hiding from the police, like our enemies think! You'll understand all this eventually.

Drumming is heard from the Bhadrakali Temple.

PARAMU NAAYAR. *Keelikottu* has started at the Bhadrakali Temple. Today's *kathakali* play is the *Killing of Duryodhana*.[52]

COMRADE'S VOICE. Bhadrakali, who killed the demon Darika, is being worshipped 'artistically' with this performance of the *Killing of Duryodhana*!

Everyone laughs. All stand up, as if they've seen the Comrade standing up. They greet him with clenched fists. They seem like shadows in a tableau. Drumming is growing louder.

Scene 3

Goopaalapilla's small Payikalil house. His wife is sitting on a bench on the veranda. She is full of anxiety and fear. A lighted lamp is on the bench. It is night. A dog barks. She reacts with shock. She picks up the lamp and goes to the door, peering outside. From the expression on her face it is clear that she has seen someone. She begins to pant. As she moves backward, Goopaalapilla enters. She puts the lamp down on the bench.

GOOPAALAPILLA'S WIFE (*anxiously*). Did you know that the police have come?

GOOPAALAPILLA. Did they come here?

WIFE. No.

---

52 *The Killing of Duryodhana* is a popular *kathakali* dance-drama which enacts a part of one of India's two great epics, the *Mahabharata*. In this play, one of the five Pandava brothers, the strong-willed Bhima, avenges the insult paid to their collective wife, Draupadi, when he disembowels Dushasana, the evil Kaurava who had attempted to publicly disrobe Draupadi at their court. In the *kathakali* version of the story, when the fight between Bhima and Dushasana occurs, the actor playing Bhima appears in his 'furious' (*raudra*) form, rips open his stomach, and washes Draupadi's hair in his blood.

GOOPAALAPILLA. But they will.

WIFE. Ayyooo.

GOOPAALAPILLA. It's rumoured that your brother and I are wanted for fishing in the public pond. We'll be in hiding for awhile. If you don't see us, don't worry. (*Goopaalapilla's wife begins to cry. He lovingly touches her head.*) Why are you so sad?

WIFE. Who is there to care for our two girls and I?

GOOPAALAPILLA. The other villagers.

WIFE. And what if you're caught by the police?

GOOPAALAPILLA. I'll be thrown in jail and tortured. I might even be killed. In the Salem jail, the police shot and killed twenty-three persons. They were in their cells when they were shot down. Another person was killed in the Thiruvananthapuram jail. The Reserve Police entered his cell and tortured him to death. Punaloor Rajagopalan lost some of his teeth. Vijayan's hand was broken. This is how they're torturing everyone.

WIFE (*crying*). I'm afraid.

GOOPAALAPILLA. You know that up to now we've been living in fear of the landlord. That has to end one day. Our children should grow up without fear. (*Both of them are silent for a few moments.*) Did the children sleep?

WIFE. Yes. They went to sleep without eating supper. They were waiting to eat with their father.

GOOPAALAPILLA (*emotionally, after a pause*). I'm beginning to think that children shouldn't be loved so much.

WIFE. How can you say that?

GOOPAALAPILLA. They love me too much. That's why they won't eat without me. When I'm not here, they go to sleep without eating. They'll be affected too much if I don't return!

WIFE. Don't even say that!

GOOPAALAPILLA. I'm only saying what might happen. But you can't worry about it. You'll have to give them my love also.

WIFE. Can a mother's love substitute for a father's?

GOOPAALAPILLA. I loved them too much. They love me more than you. I'm afraid all that will result in endless sorrow. (*Goopaalapilla stands still with sorrow. His wife cries.*)

GOOPAALAPILLA (*after taking a long breath*). Perhaps I'll kiss the children. It may be my last chance.

Goopaalapilla enters the house. His wife stands alone. Just before he goes inside, a dog starts barking continuously. He goes to the door and looks out. His wife is also anxious.

WIFE. Someone is coming. Four or five persons.

GOOPAALAPILLA (*looking out*). Don't be afraid. It's not the police.

Paramu Naayar, Kunnuraaman, Parameeswaran Naayar, Raaghavan, and others enter.

PARAMU NAAYAR (*turning back*). Why is Teevan standing back? Come in! (*Teevan enters, aware that he belongs to the lowest class and staying aloof from the others. Everyone else sits down on the bench or the floor. Teevan sits apart. Looking at Goopaalapilla's Wife*) Sister, do you have anything to eat? We're hungry.

GOOPAALAPILLA WIFE. There's some *puzhuke* with tapioca, *kachil* and *kizhangngu*. We only have enough rice for the children.

GOOPAALAPILLA. Bring the *puzhuke*[53] in a dish. None of us have eaten all day. Before we leave we can each have a few pieces and drink some water.

PARAMU NAAYAR. Keep the rice for the children when they wake up.

Goopaalapilla's Wife goes inside.

KUNNURAAMAN (*to Goopaalapilla*). The police and the landlord's goondas are in the market. We don't know what they're planning.

PARAMU NAAYAR. Maybe they're going to search our homes. The landlord's goondas will identify which homes to search.

KUNNURAAMAN. We should be ready. If they attack our houses, we should counter-attack with stones and force them back.

RAAGHAVAN. There's bright moonlight tonight.

PARAMU NAAYAR. We'll be able to target what we throw.

Everyone laughs.

GOOPAALAPILLA. That goonda, Nannu Naayar, is a poisonous worm.

PARAMU NAAYAR. If he's the one who identifies our houses, let's attack him.

KUNNURAAMAN. The Vallikunnam goonda organization 'dis-organized'

53 *Puzhuke* is a preparation of mixed vegetables.

itself! DSP, with the help of the landlords, organized the group and called it a 'voluntary organization!' At a meeting DSP called for everyone there willing to join the 'voluntary organization' to raise their hands. Only five or six raised their hands. Then DSP declared that those who hadn't raised their hands would be 'dealt with.' So a few more raised their hands. So now they're 'dis-organized!'

RAAGHAVAN. Why is that?

KUNNURAAMAN. We have noted exactly who the major goondas are, and we've 'dealt with them' severely. They say that police torture is better than ours! (*Everyone laughs.*) Those who were beaten left the organization voluntarily. But we failed to catch one. His home was set afire.

TEEVAN. You didn't have to set fire to his house!

KUNNURAAMAN. There's no way for us to survive unless we threaten these goondas!

Goopaalapilla's wife brings a bamboo dish of cooked tapioca with pepper chutney. All sit in a circle and eat. Teevan is still sitting apart.

KUNNURAAMAN. Come and join us here.

TEEVAN. I can sit here, Comrade.

KUNNURAAMAN. How can you eat *puzhuke* if you sit over there? Come and sit here. (*Teevan comes and eats with everyone else.*)

GOOPAALAPILLA. If there's any rice water, could you bring it?

GOOPAALAPILLA'S WIFE. Is it possible to get much rice water when you can only cook a small measure of rice?

PARAMU NAAYAR. Plain water is enough.

Goopaalapilla's Wife goes inside.

RAAGHAVAN. Comrade Kunnuraaman should tell us what happened at Vallikkunnath.

KUNNURAAMAN. You can pull that trick on yourself! If I talk you'll be able to eat everything! So you can tell what happened there. (*Eats some tapioca to emphasize the joke as everyone laughs.*)

PARAMU NAAYAR (*while eating*). Once there were two people who were eating from the same dish. The first one asked the second one, 'How did your mother die?' As soon as he was asked, he began to feel sad as he remembered how his mother had died. So he stopped eating, and began to cry while he narrated how good his mother had been, and went on to describe her disease, and eventual death. While the second one was telling this long story, the first one had eaten three-fourths of the food. Only when he finished his long story did the second one realize the secret of this cunning question. Thinking he could still manage to eat the rest of the food, the second one asked the first, 'How did *your* mother die?' But without pausing, the first one replied quickly, 'Oh, she vomitted and died.' Kunnuraaman can't be fooled like that!

Everyone laughs. A dog barks outside. They stop eating suddenly and listen. Goopaalapilla's wife enters with the water, stands still, and looks outside. Some of them still have food in their hands. Some have stopped chewing. One man still has his hand in the dish. A tableau. Someone enters from outside, panting heavily.

PARAMU NAAYAR. What?

NEWCOMER. The police have started searching houses. First they went into Kalakkattu Thara. The oldest one in the family was severely tortured. He was bedridden, but the police just grabbed his legs and head and dragged him outside into the compound. There they beat him!

Everyone is in shock with panic.

KUNNURAAMAN. Where did they go next?

NEWCOMER. To Ceennan Pulayan's home.

TEEVAN (*anxiously*). Did they beat father?

NEWCOMER. They beat and kicked him continuously! Then . . . (*unable to continue*) . . .

GOOPAALAPILLA. What happened?

The new comer remains silent.

KUNNURAAMAN. Comrade, tell us what happened.

NEWCOMER. Two or three of the goondas caught Teevan's wife and dragged her away.

TEEVAN (*jumps up anxiously*). I'm going! (*Starts to run off.*)

KUNNURAAMAN (*catching Teevan*). You can't go alone and start something! We're coming too!!

A dog barks continuously. Parameeswaran Naayar jumps up. The others wait anxiously.

PARAMU NAAYAR (*running to the veranda anxiously*). It's the police!

Everyone jumps up. Some start to run away.

KUNNURAAMAN. No one should run off alone! Hide along the roadside by this house. (*Pointing to the back*) Run this way!

All run out to the back of the house one by one. Frightened, Goopaalapilla's Wife takes the bamboo dish and runs inside. The dog continues to bark. The sound of boots marching. A few moments later Nannu Naayar enters with a uniformed policeman. The policeman carries a gun, and Nannu Naayar a torch. Goopaalapilla's Wife enters, afraid.

NANNU NAAYAR. Where's Goopaalapilla?

GOOPAALAPILLA'S WIFE. He went out this morning. I don't know where he is.

NANNU NAAYAR. Where is Parameeswaran?

GOOPAALAPILLA'S WIFE. He too left this morning.

NANNU NAAYAR. Have Paramu, Teevan, or Raaghavan come here?

GOOPAALAPILLA'S WIFE. No, no one has come.

NANNU NAAYAR (*to the policeman*). You can't believe anything these communist women say! Once near Alappuzha in a local ward, the Reserve Police were trying to discover a cell. S. Kumaran, one of the culprits in the Punnapra-Vayalar case, was hiding in one of the local huts. He convinced a mother to accompany him with her baby. He carried the infant on his shoulder, and the mother went with him carrying an empty bottle for medicine.[54] When Kumaran and the woman approached the police, they said, 'The baby is seriously ill. We're taking it to the hospital.' Then they pinched the baby so that it starting wailing. And then the mother also started crying. So the policeman said, 'Go on and hurry to the hospital!' This is how the one called 'S' escaped. So don't believe her either! Go and search inside! (*Gives him the torch. The policeman goes inside. In a moment, a child cries out loudly.*)

GOOPAALAPILLA'S WIFE. Ayyoo! My child's being kicked! (*She runs inside.*)

NANNU NAAYAR (*grabbing her by her wrist*). Where are you going! The child's crying out in her sleep.

Two children are heard crying.

GOOPAALAPILLA'S WIFE (*trying to free herself*). No, no, my children are being kicked! (*She continues to struggle to escape.*)

POLICEMAN. Hey, quit making so much noise. My superior is waiting

---

54 During this period, if someone had to go to a doctor they carried their own empty bottles into which medicine could be poured to take home.

outside the compound! Take her there!
(*The Policeman grabs her other arm, and the two of them drag her outside. She cries out. The children cry from inside the house.*)

INSPECTOR'S VOICE (offstage). Chi! Stop crying! (*Goopaalapilla's Wife's crying stops as if she's become frightened. The children's weak sobs can still be heard.*) Come here!

GOOPAALAPILLA'S WIFE (*offstage*). Ayyoo! Sir, let go of me! Let go! I'm a mother with two small children! Tamburaan, free me!

Goondas and policemen laugh. The children cry from inside.

A MAN'S SHOUT. I've been hit by a stone on the head! Somebody's throwing them!

Sounds of stones falling on the roof of the house.

INSPECTOR'S VOICE. Where'd the stones come from? Ready! Fire!

POLICEMAN'S VOICE. It's impossible to tell!

INSPECTOR'S VOICE. Fire! (*A shot is heard.*)

POLICEMAN'S VOICE. Quick, let's get out of here!

ANOTHER VOICE. Ayyoo! My head's been hit!

Nannu Naayar races onto the veranda in fear, and goes running out in the opposite direction. More sounds of stones being thrown.

INSPECTOR'S VOICE. Where are our guides!

POLICEMAN'S VOICE. They ran off in different directions. Let's get out of here too!

The sound of running. Goopaalapilla's wife runs onto the veranda from the compound. Her hair is loose, and she's frightened. The children are crying. Parameeswaran Naayar runs in from the back of the house..

GOOPAALAPILLA'S WIFE (*crying*). Ayyoo! Where's my husband?
(*Parameeswaran Naayar, without listening to his sister, runs into the house. She follows him. The children cry. Parameeswaran Naayar comes back out with a hatchet. His sister chases him and catches him by the arm.*) Ayyoo! Don't! Don't! (*They fight over the hatchet.*)

PARAMU NAAYAR (*sharply and loudly*). Let me go! Stay here where it's safe!

He frees himself from her grip and runs out. She bursts into tears and looks offstage. From outside, the sounds of the clash between the police and comrades can be heard.

Scene 4

Ripe paddy fields. Shadows reflecting the fight between the police and common people. The sounds of kathakali *drumming from the nearby temple. A series of offstage voices/cries are heard.*

#1: Women should be able to live in peace in our country!
#2: Ayyoo!
#3: We won't live as slaves anymore!

INSPECTOR'S VOICE. Ayyoo! Let go of me! Let go! Don't kill me!

PARAMU NAAYAR'S VOICE. We'll end the tyranny of the landlords. We won't bend to his yoke anymore!

#4: Kill him!
#5: No! Don't!
#3: Don't let him go!

The shadow of a policeman running with a gun. A man chases him and snatches his gun. A confrontation.

VOICE. Get his gun!

One comrade wrestles away his gun. The policeman runs. The comrade chases him. From the paddy field there are sounds of fighting everywhere. Dogs bark and snarl.[55] *The Inspector runs followed by Teevan and others.*

TEEVAN'S VOICE. You spoiled my Niili! You'll pay for this!

The Inspector and his followers exit.

VOICE. Ayyooo!

PARAMU NAAYAR. This is the burial ground of slavery! A few lives must be sacrificed here. First you! Then us!

The drumming comes to an end at the temple.

The Killing of Duryodhana *is over.*

The sounds of the fighting gradually decrease and end. The snarling and barking of dogs increase. Perfect silence.

55 In traditional folk belief, the snarling of a dog is read as a sign of an abnormal, often violent death. Bhaasi's use of the snarling dog here politicizes this folk belief.

Scene 5

In front of Goopaalapilla's house. Goopaalapilla's Wife is sobbing as if she's witnessed all these events. She covers her eyes with her hands. Goopaalapilla enters, panting. He's tired. His wife takes away her hands. There are blood stains on his shirt.

GOOPAALAPILLA'S WIFE (*crying*). This didn't have to happen! It didn't have to happen!

GOOPAALAPILLA (*exhausted and heartbroken*). It had to be done!

WIFE. No! It didn't have to happen!

GOOPAALAPILLA. There's no use saying it again. I've come to say goodbye to you and the children.

WIFE. Where will you go?

GOOPAALAPILLA. I don't know. I'll try to escape, but if I can't, this is my last visit. (*He crosses to the door of the house to look at the children. He loses his courage and turns back. To his wife*) Please, care for the children. (*She faints. He slowly walks away. A dog snarls from a distance.*)

ACT FOUR

Scene 1

A deserted village road. A junction. The shops are closed. The silence is broken by the lowing of a cow.[56] *The sound of the marching feet of the Reserve Police comes closer, and then goes away in a different direction. An announcement is heard from a microphone. The sound of a jeep.*

ANNOUNCEMENT. Last night a sub-inspector and four policemen were killed by the communists. From today, January 1, 1950 onward, the Communist Party, their labour organizations, and any related organizations are banned! We hereby declare that in Suranad and the surrounding areas ACT 144 is in force. Curfew is in order, and public meetings are banned.

The announcement is heard moving further away. In order to hear the announcement clearly, the landlord and Nannu Naayar enter from the right. They are clearly happy. The announcement continues:

Giving shelter to communists is a punishable offense. Rewards will be offered to anyone providing information about, or capturing dead or alive any of the following: Sankaran Narayanan Thambi, Thooppil Bhaasi, and anyone else directly involved in the Suranad murders!

NANNU NAAYAR (*casts a meaningful glance at the landlord. The announcement fades away.*) They should have done this a long time ago!

JANMI. This will bring an end to the story of communism.

Nannu Naayar laughs. The lowing of a cow.

NANNU NAAYAR. The cattle are still in their sheds. All the villagers ran away.

JANMI. I heard that this morning, a number of chickens and goats were picked up and taken to the Reserve Police camp in Poika Plains.

The lowing of a cow.

NANNU NAAYAR. When the chicken and goats are finished, they'll put an end to the lowing of the cows. They're certainly enjoying all 'amenities'.

---

56 According to traditional folk belief, the lowing of a cow can be read as indicating spiritual sterility or starvation.

JANMI (*smiling*). Meat's readily available here for eating and for 'pleasure.'

NANNU NAAYAR (*doesn't quite catch his meaning*). What do you mean 'for pleasure?' (*The landlord smiles and looks at Nannu Naayar meaningfully.*) Oh, I get it! After ten months there will be many new soldier 'kids' and police 'kids.'

JANMI. They haven't suffered enough. They're revolting against tenancy and landlordism. Bhaasi's home was confiscated. His father was arrested, locked up, and tortured. During the torturing he vomitted blood. His mother is wandering around the streets. None of her relatives would take her in. Everything including their furniture and utensils was carted off in a van—even their cattle!

The lowing of a cow.

NANNU NAAYAR. The cattle's condition is getting pitiful! Do you hear their lowing? Do the police feed the cattle? You know, even though his father was arrested, Bhaasi hasn't turned himself in to the police.

JANMI. No, he hasn't. But they'll find him. They're offering a handsome reward for his head and that of their leader.

NANNU NAAYAR (*coughs*). If I had seen him, I would have been able to climb out of my poverty. I could've had my cough treated. But I can't catch them. It's said they are armed with pistols. But I can point them out. Would I get a reward for that?

JANMI. It's enough to provide information that leads to their arrest.

NANNU NAAYAR. I can do that. (*Thinking*) But they're clever and cunning enough to trick the police. One day M. N., the one who escaped from jail, fell into a trap the police set. But he escaped. Do you know how? He saw someone carrying a bundle of hay on his head. M. N. bought the bundle, and then carried it on his head, and simply walked away! You know how you can only see someone's legs when they're carrying a huge bundle of hay. If you're only looking at someone's legs you can't tell whether he's a communist or a Congressman. So M. N. walked out right under the noses of the police!

JANMI. But T.V. and Sugathan who are equally 'clever' have ended up eating from the mud pot in the jail! Now that the party is banned, the police are discovering them without much difficulty.

NANNU NAAYAR. I'm sure the police will find them all.

JANMI. It's still early morning, but already Thandasserry, Kalakkattutara Parameeswaran, and two or three others have been arrested.

NANNU NAAYAR. Payikkatt Parameeswaran and Paramu haven't been arrested yet. They're the key.

JANMI. Don't worry about them. They'll all be caught eventually. The Reserve Police has set up its camp here.

NANNU NAAYAR. Oh yes, they'll be caught. These 'flat-hatters' aren't like the 'pointed-hatters!'[57] They've got a lot of energy. They'll catch them! (*The sound of a jeep coming from off left. The landlord and Nannu Naayar look in that direction.*) A jeep. It's the Reserve Police! (*The sound of a jeep arriving and stopping. The sound of a lathi charge from off left. Shouts from the left* 'Ayyoo! Ayyoo!' 'I don't know!' 'Don't beat me.' *Other screams and shouts. Women are also heard crying.*) Everyone's running in a different direction! Look! Some of them are falling down! The police are kicking some of them while they're down! (*Laughs.*)

JANMI. Let them suffer!

NANNU NAAYAR. They have to suffer. They've become too proud!

Both men and women run on from the left, and cross offstage to the right. Ceennan rushes in. He's been viciously tortured. He's crying and panting.

CEENNAN. Oh great Tamburaan-lord, please save us! (*He kneels down before the landlord.*)

NANNU NAAYAR. Don't touch him! You'll make him impure! Stay over there and say what you want, old Pulaya!

CEENNAN (*raising his head, he looks pathetically at the landlord's face*). Last night and this morning, I've been kicked and beaten by the police. I can't even work anymore. Now they've caught Teevan and taken him to Poika Plains where they're beating and kicking him. Tamburaan-lord, please save him before they kill him!

JANMI. What can be done for someone who's killed the police?

CEENNAN. He didn't kill anyone. If they think he did it, then they should put him in jail. Just ask them not to torture him to death!

JANMI. I won't ask.

CEENNAN. Until this moment, I've never asked you for anything. I began service to your house at the age of eight and began to feed your cattle and clean the cow-shed. When I was old enough to hold a spade I started cutting the soil. I didn't even appeal to you when I saw my own father, Chattan, laying sunken in a muddy field killed by the

57 A humorous reference to the fact that the Reserve Police wear easily identifiable flat hats, and the regular police at the time wore cone-shaped pointed hats. Also a reference to the relative incompetence and lack of discipline and experience of the regular police when compared to the more disciplined Reserve Police.

great Tamburaan, your father! I stood aside and cried, but never said one word. Last night, Teevan's wife was dragged off by your wrestler and the police. (*He cries*) This morning she came back to our hut like a mad woman! But still I didn't come to you to ask anything! Now, I ask you one last time, don't let my son be tortured to death. Tamburaan-lord should simply say this to the police.

JANMI (*firmly*). No, I won't. It's nothing to me if they kill him!

CEENNAN (*in a loud voice, as if exploding*). Tamburaan! (*He stares at the landlord and stands up straight. The landlord is puzzled by the expression on his face. Nannu Naayar becomes afraid. Ceennan stares at him for a moment. In a firm declaration*) I no longer have a Tamburaan! I am no longer a slave!! (*Stares at him, and slowly walks out, exiting.*)

NANNU NAAYAR. Even that old Pulayan is raising his 'hood'.[58]

JANMI. All those 'rising hoods' will be struck down. When the Chief Minister was standing in my house compound this morning he told the police that we don't need a place like Suranad.

NANNU NAAYAR. That means around here we only need aristocratic Tamburaans like you and your followers like me. (*Surprised*) Did you see how that Ceennan looked you in the eyes? Even I, your bodyguard, got scared! So he's become a communist. But he too will be caught!

JANMI. They'll catch him. That's precisely what the Reserve Police have camped here for.

NANNU NAAYAR. Yes, they'll catch him. They're energetic. (*Looking off left*) Here's one now. (*Loudly*) Reserve-sir, come here! The Tamburaan is calling you. (*To landlord*) Tell him about Ceennan.

The landlord and Nannu Naayar look in the direction of the Reserve Police. Nannu Naayar bows when he enters.

POLICEMAN (*seriously*). Hum, what do you want?

NANNU NAAYAR (*introducing the landlord*). This is the landlord of this house. The Chief Minister came here this morning. He took coffee here.

POLICEMAN. So what?

NANNU NAAYAR. I'm just informing you. Tamburaan is a Congressman.

POLICEMAN. And who are you?

NANNU NAAYAR. I'm his 'bodyguard.' I also went with the police to point out the huts of the communists.

POLICEMAN. Ohhh! You too?

58 Like a cobra ready to strike.

NANNU NAAYAR. Yes.

POLICEMAN. Then why weren't you stabbed to death like the others?

NANNU NAAYAR. When they started throwing stones from all sides, I ran away. I know all the pathways very well. And I had a torch.

POLICEMAN. So you ran away, escaped the stone attack, and left the policemen to die?

NANNU NAAYAR. Don't joke like that!

POLICEMAN. So you betrayed the police? You helped them to kill the police?

NANNU NAAYAR (*scared*). Don't say that, Sir. What will everyone else think when they hear you joking like this.

POLICEMAN (*to the landlord*). Sir, you may go. I'm taking him to the camp.

NANNU NAAYAR (*as if crying*). Ayyooo!

POLICEMAN (*to the landlord, in a rough tone*). You better go. He must be questioned.

NANNU NAAYAR. Ayyoo! Don't go, Tamburaan. (*The landlord walks away without turning back. Crying*) Tamburaan! Take me with you or I'll be killed. Tamburaan!

POLICEMAN. Chii! Shut up! (*landlord exits.*)

NANNU NAAYAR. Tamburaan!

POLICEMAN (*slapping him on the cheek*). Bastard! You consented to have the policemen killed!

NANNU NAAYAR. I didn't know anything! Save me! I'm a 'coughing' patient.

POLICEMAN. I'll 'save' you. (*Catches him by the pants around his stomach and hustles him off to the left. He gives him a swift kick in the rear as he is about to exit. Nannu Naayar falls down. The policeman kicks him several more times. Then he pulls him up.*) You can have the rest when you reach camp. Now march!

The Policeman exits with Nannu Naayar. A cow is heard lowing in the distance.

Scene 2

Inside a jail cell. The iron gate is stage left. Through the door, the movements of the police can be seen. Paramu Naayar, Teevan, Kunnuraaman and seven or eight other prisoners look out through the iron bars. Kunnuraaman and Paramu Naayar both are feeling anger and anxiety. Teevan and others are simply afraid. Two of those who have been tortured are lying on the floor. One man is crying out in pain. Another is leaning against the wall. All the prisoners wear a single dhoti or coloured lungi. A pot in the corner of the room for urinating. The walls are stained with the blood of mosquitoes and bugs. The sound of one man being tortured can be heard from outside. It's reflected in the faces of the prisoners.

PRISONER (*on the floor*). Water. Water! (*Kunnuraaman goes to him.*) Water.

Kunnuraaman crosses to the bars and looks out.

KUNNURAAMAN. Clerk! This dying man is crying out for water. Give me a glass of water!

POLICEMAN VOICE. Urinate in his mouth!

KUNNURAAMAN. Phaa . . . bastard! (*Looking at him fiercely*).

PARAMU NAAYAR. Filthy bitch!

POLICEMAN (*coming to the bars*). You're next!

PARAMU NAAYAR. Yes, I know. Right now you're torturing Payikkat Goopaalapilla in the Inspector's office. We can hear it! Sure, after that, we're next!

INSPECTOR'S VOICE (*off*). Take him out of here and put him in the hall where everyone inside can see him.

Everyone inside looks out. The sound of four or five persons walking in boots.

TEEVAN (*with extreme sorrow*). Goopaalapilla's being taken out.

INSPECTOR'S VOICE. Throw him on the floor! (*Sound of man falling to the floor. Those inside the cell are shocked.*) Even though he's been tortured, he didn't reveal anything, didn't even make a sound—not even one 'ayyoo.' He should be killed.

PARAMU NAAYAR (*at the height of his anger*). Kill him! Kill him, street bitches!! You won't even find the word 'ayyoo' in our dictionary! We're revolutionaries!

KUNNURAAMAN. When you arrested Puthupalli Raaghavan and Peroor Madhavan, you stopped the van at each junction, took them in chains out of the van, and tortured them in public. You made it a street performance of police torture. But did they cry 'ayyoo?'

INSPECTOR'S VOICE. To free them Bhaasi and others attacked the Kayamkulam Police Station. The leader escaped, but he was naked!

TEEVAN. Still, he escaped!

KUNNURAAMAN. Comrade Bhaasi ran ten kilometres naked at night and found shelter before dawn. In the Klappana a Muslim family gave him shelter—a Muslim everyone called 'friend.' Some people started to gather around that hut since they thought a rich young Muslim was hiding a woman there. So Bhaasi told them to reveal the fact that it was he who was in hiding. One friend revealed that it was Bhaasi. When they learned who it was, they all left quietly. So all that day they guarded him.

PARAMU NAAYAR. Yes, some of us will be caught, but most of us will be protected by our people.

INSPECTOR'S VOICE. Chi! Shut up! Otherwise you can be tortured right now!

PARAMU NAAYAR. Sure! You can kill us all! You murdered Thandasserry Raaghavan the day he was caught! Kalakkattutara Parameeswaran Naayar was dead within a month! Chalithara Kunjachan was murdered. Raman Naayar was killed. Payikkalil Goopaalapilla is being tortured and put outside to die. It's our turn next!

INSPECTOR'S VOICE. Didn't all of you conspire and kill an inspector and four policemen?

KUNNURAAMAN. Yes, inspector. And didn't the soldiers who came to Cochin during World War II rape our native women? Gandhi knew this and told his Congressmen, 'You may not have guns, but you have your teeth and nails!' We've done nothing to transgress Gandhi's preachings on non-violence. We only killed with our own 'weapons' those who came with guns to rape our women!

TEEVAN. You spoiled my Niili!

PARAMU NAAYAR. Yes, police were killed in the encounter. We're sorry about that. We didn't kill *them* by first arresting them, throwing them in jail, and then taking them out one-by-one with their hands and legs tied together!

KUNNURAAMAN. If you have the courage, let us all out and try to kill us together. We can count the statistics of the dead later.

INSPECTOR'S VOICE. Chi! Just shut up!

PARAMU NAAYAR. Our voices will be heard even after we die. They are the voices of revolution.

INSPECTOR'S VOICE. Revolution! Your revolution. I'll make you shout, 'Short Live the Revolution!'

KUNNURAAMAN. You will never make us do that, inspector. Those who aren't in jail will only be hanged if they've been fraudulently sentenced. Until we die we'll shout, 'Long Live the Revolution,' and 'An End to Slavery!'

INSPECTOR'S VOICE. Constable! Make the one lying here call out, 'Short Live the Revolution!'

POLICEMAN'S VOICE. Say, 'Short Live the Revolution.'

GOOPAALAPILLA (*in a weak voice*). No, I won't say that.

INSPECTOR'S VOICE. Goopaalapilla, if you want to live, say 'Short Live the Revolution.'

GOOPAALAPILLA'S VOICE. 'Long Live the Revolution.'

Those who are in the jail cell repeat his chant.

INSPECTOR'S VOICE. If you want to see your children again, say 'Short Live the Revolution.'

GOOPAALAPILLA'S VOICE. My only wish was to kiss my children once more before my death. But I can't. I heard that when you interrogated my wife, you plunged my two-and-a-half year old daughter, Leela, under water. When she struggled and began to suffocate, you took her out, and then repeated it again and again. Finally, you 'insulted' my wife, didn't you, Inspector!

INSPECTOR'S VOICE. Constable, put your boot on his neck and push until he cries out, 'Short Live the Revolution!'

GOOPAALAPILLA'S VOICE. 'Long Live the Revolution. An End to Slavery. Long Live the Rev . . . ' (*the sound of his struggle and suffocation.*)

Those in the cell are watching with anger and anguish. Teevan sobs openly as he sees Goopaalapilla dying outside the cell.

PARAMU NAAYAR. Don't cry. It will shame the martyrdom of Goopaalapilla. Let's shout with one voice the words locked in his throat, 'Long Live the Revolution!'

Everyone repeats the slogan, following Paramu Naayar. The prisoner who is close to death on the floor also raises his fist.

PARAMU NAAYAR. 'An End to Slavery.' (*Everyone repeats.*) 'Long Live the Revolution.' (*Everyone repeats.*)

CONCLUDING WORDS (*BHARATAVAAKYAM*)[59]

The Stage Manager enters, and bows to the audience.

STAGE MANAGER. The concept of Kerala State has become a reality. On our soil slavery has been exterminated. The system of tenure is being brought to an end. Those who were in hiding have come out. The jails have been opened. Political activists should be selfless and radiant in their sacrifice. These are the 'concluding words' for this historical play you've seen.

(*Looking offstage*) All those who performed, please come to the stage. We will sing a poem by Vayalar Rama Varma, as our final 'Concluding Words.'

The actors and actresses come to the stage from both sides. Together they sing the Bharatavaakyam.

SONG:

Haven't you seen this—this was a new message to the Land of Kerala.

It was the proud proclamation of the Keralites' concept of culture.

It was the slashing of the Day's sword against the gathering darkness which nurtures the past.

It was a terrible warning for all those who would dishonour the land.

It was the war cry of the people who blew the victory conch announcing the culture's new age.

It was the cry of the possessed.

The life-breath of youth—this tornado has traversed all domains through the ages.

---

59 Like the *nandi*, a convention taken from Sanskrit drama.

APPENDIX

Caste, Land, and Reform in Kerala

Phillip B. Zarrilli

Since issues of the relationship between the traditional caste structure, the right to hold land and therefore have access to land-based wealth, and socio-political reforms which challenged traditional assumptions and relationships between caste, land, and relationships in service are central to *Memories in Hiding*, the following brief account of these issues in Kerala is appended, especially for the reader unfamiliar with Kerala. This brief account is *not* intended to be complete or definitive, but to identify issues and relationships, and to suggest the relative hierarchy, ranking, and relationships assumed and challenged in *Memories in Hiding*.[60]

Regarding Caste

Most sources generally agree with the following ordering of castes, listed by 'decreasing' status and by higher degree of 'pollution.'

Non-polluting high castes

Namboodiri Brahmins
Landlords of larger estates
Lower sub-castes owning smaller estates, temple priests, physicians, household priests, cooks
Other foreign Brahmins
Kshatriyas
Samantans (and other titled royal lineages of Naayars)
Ambalavasis (temple servants)
Naayars (includes estate and house owners)
Middle ranking retainers (including lower ranking Naayars)

---

60 For a more complete account of the caste structure of traditional Kerala which informs the revolutionary movement of the period of the Suranad rebellion staged in this play, consult the following studies: C. J. Fuller (*The Nayars Today*. London: Cambridge University Press, 1976), Robin Jeffrey (*The Decline of Nayar Dominance*. Sussex: Sussex University Press, 1976), J. Puthenkalam (*Marriage and the Family in Kerala*. Calgary: University of Calgary Department of Sociology, *Journal of Comparative Family Studies*, 1977), Kathleen Gough ('Nayar: Central Kerala,' in Kathleen Gough and David M. Schneider, *Matrilineal Kinship*, 298-404. Berkeley: University of California Press, 1961; also 'Changing Kinship Usages in the Setting of Political and Economic Change Among the Nayars of Malabar,' *Journal of Royal Anthropological Institute*, 82, Pt. I, 71-88, 1952), and Melinda Moore, 'Taravad: House, Land and Relationship in Matrilineal Hindu Society,' unpublished Ph.D. dissertation, University of Chicago, 1983.

Various specific lower ranking sub-groups including those serving in Brahmin kitchens, servants to Namboodiris and rulers, bearers, washermen, barbers and midwives, or funeral priests (including lower ranking Naayars)

Higher polluting castes

Kammalas (artisan castes including carpenters, stone-carvers, blacksmiths, brass and coppersmiths, and goldsmiths)

Tiyyas, Izhavas, or Thandans
Chovans (tenant farmers, toddy tappers)
Kaniyans (astrologers and agricultural labourers)

Lower polluting castes

Mukkuvans and Aryans (fishermen)
Pulayas or Cherumans (Harijan castes)
Parayas

Within the play, there are a number of variously ranking Naayars, each belonging to a different subcaste, and therefore each of a different rank. For example, Nannu Naayar, who is in service to the landlord, often called Tamburaan or *janmi*, defines himself as a lower ranking Thoruvakkaran Naayar in contrast to the Tamburaan who 'belongs to the noble line of Pillais!'

The Basic Socio-Economic Unit, 'House and Land'

The socio-economic structure which organized relationships between and among castes until the demise of this system in the twentieth century was the fundamental unit, 'house and land'.[61] The right to hold land was only in possession of the highest ranking non-polluting castes—Namboodiri Brahmins, the royal lineages (including a few Kshatriya groups and the highest-ranking title-holding Naayars, often called Samantans), lesser ranking Naayar chiefs (*naduvaaris*) and/or village heads (*desavaaris*), and temples.[62] Those with the right to hold land did so by birth right (*janmam*). The majority of those working and living on the land did so by tenure (*kanam*), in service to those holding *janmam* rights over them.[63]

The basic unit, 'house and land,' was ideally intended to be a self-sufficient microcosm, designed to contain a more or less complete set of

61 Moore, 1983, 273; Eric J. Miller, 'Caste and Territory in Malabar,' *American Anthropologist*, 1954:56, 410-20; Eric J. Miller, 'Village Structure in North Kerala,' *India's Villages*, ed. M. N. Srinivas (N.Y.: Asia Publishing House, 1955); Joan P. Mencher, 'Namboodiri Brahmins: An Analysis of a Traditional Elite in Kerala,' *Journal of Asian and African Studies* (1966: 1, 3, 183-196).
62 Puthenkalam, 1977, 14.
63 Moore, 1983, 281ff.; Gough, 1961, 308-9.

> the beings inhabiting the universe and the entire set of life-cycle events of persons who are its members . . . [T]he rest of society seems to remain solitary by means of a set of ritual relationships defined relative to it.[64]

The ideal microcosm (house and land) was only realized by those at the very top of the hierarchy, Namboodiri Brahmins, the aristocratic Kshatriya or Naayar ruling lineages, or large temples dedicated to pan-Indian puranic deities. Each house and its land provided for not merely subsistence, but the conduct of cultural activities (temple maintenance, festivals); and was not satisfied merely with things, but required persons of all kinds (i.e., *jatis*) who were either granted along with the land (e.g., the Cerumans) or encouraged to settle on it (e.g., the Izhavas and artisans).[65]

The landlord in the play is often identified as '*janmi*,' i.e., he who holds birth right to rule over those in his service. Since he belongs to a 'noble line of Pillai' Naayars, he holds the right to own land and serve as landlord to those in service to his household.

Leftist Politics and Land Reform

One of the primary goals of communist reformists and revolutionaries was land reform, since it was at the heart of the traditional feudal *janmi* system of socio-economic relationships.[66] When the CPI came to power in Kerala in the 1957 election as it collected 35 percent of the votes and won 60 of 125 seats up for election,[67] it immediately introduced the Agrarian Relations Bill. However, it was not passed until 1961 in a form modified 'to accomodate land interests' with the Congress-PSP ministry in office. Nevertheless, it was 'the first comprehensive measure of its kind attempted in India' and a self-conscious attempt by the CPI to abolish feudalism.[68]

---

64 Melinda Moore, 'Nalukettu: The House as Microcosm,' unpublished paper presented at the 11th Annual Conference on South Asia, Madison, Wisconsin, 1982.

65 Moore, 1983, 142.

66 Regarding the complicated history of land reform in Kerala, in addition to Nossiter (1982, 1988), see also Henry C. Hart and Ronald J. Herring, 'Political Conditions of Land Reform: Kerala and Maharashtra,' in *Land Tenure and Peasant in South Asia*, ed. Robert E. Frykenberg (Delhi, 1977), and Ronald J. Herring, 'Abolition of Land-lordism in Kerala: A Redistribution of Privilege,' *Economic and Political Weekly*, 15, 2 (June 28, 1980).

67 T. J. Nossiter,1988, 65 and 1982, 123.

68 Nossiter 1982, 149-50.